Using CRC Cards

ADVANCES IN OBJECT TECHNOLOGY SERIES

Dr. Richard S. Wiener
Series Editor

Editor
Journal of Object-Oriented Programming
Report on Object Analysis and Design
SIGS Publications, Inc.
New York, New York

and

Department of Computer Science
University of Colorado
Colorado Springs, Colorado

Additional Volumes in Preparation

Using CRC Cards

An Informal Approach to Object-Oriented Development

Nancy M. Wilkinson

AT&T Bell Laboratories

SIGS BOOKS
New York

Library of Congress Cataloging-in-Publication Data

Wilkinson, Nancy M., 1956-
    Using CRC Cards : an informal approach to object-oriented
    development / Nancy M. Wilkinson.
        p.   cm. -- (Advances in object technology ; 6)
    Includes bibliographical references.
    ISBN 1-884842-07-0 (acid free paper)
    1. Object-oriented programming (Computer science)   I. Title.
II. Series.
QA76.63.W55 1995
005.1'1--dc20   95-3987
                                                                      CIP

PUBLISHED BY
SIGS Books
71 W. 23rd Street, Third Floor
New York, New York 10010

SIGS Books ISBN 1-884842-07-0
Prentice Hall ISBN 0-13-374679-8

Printed in the United States of America
99 98 97 96 95   10 9 8 7 6 5 4 3 2 1
First Printing April 1995

To Liz,
for a lifetime of love and laughter

About the Author

Nancy M. Wilkinson, an expert in the use of C++ and object-oriented design, has been with AT&T Bell Laboratories since 1979. In her current position with the Software Development Technology Group, Wilkinson has led an object-oriented design and programming consulting effort within AT&T. She developed a CRC card course and company wide C++ programming guidelines. She has also developed tools to transition C to C++ code and to ensure compliance with C++ coding standards. Prior to this, Wilkinson was a member of the Languages Tools group in Bell Labs. There, she was a part of the cfront development team for AT&T C++ Language Releases 2.1 and 3.0. She has had numerous titles published in technical journals and magazines, including *C++ Report*, and she writes a column for *Report on Object Analysis and Design* (SIGS Publications). She has also given CRC card workshops at numerous conferences, such as Object Expo and C++ World.

Wilkinson received a bachelor's degree in mathematics from Gettysburg College, Gettysburg, Pennsylvania, and a master's degree in computer science from Stevens Institute of Technology, Hoboken, New Jersey.

Series Introduction

$\mathcal{T}$HE Advances in Object Technology series seeks to present readers with books that provide incisive and timely information relating to object-oriented programming and programming languages, object-oriented requirements, object-oriented domain analysis, and object-oriented design. In addition, testing, metrics, formal methods and applications of object technology to areas including object-oriented databases, real-time systems, emergent computation, neural networks, and object-oriented distributed systems will be featured. The books are aimed at practicing software development professionals, programmers, educators, and students in computer-related disciplines.

Using CRC Cards is an important book. Nancy Wilkinson's years of experience at AT&T Bell Labs have provided the practical experience in using C++ and designing object-oriented systems that comes through in this book. Her superb writing skills make this a most pleasurable book to read. Even if you consider yourself an experienced C++ programmer, you will benefit tremendously from the insight that Nancy Wilkinson presents relating CRC analysis and design to C++ implementation. Relatively little has been written about CRC analysis and design, although it is a widely used and important process. I believe that this book will emerge as a classic for anyone interested in this important technique.

Richard S. Wiener
Series Editor

Foreword

Dᴇsɪɢɴᴇʀs ᴡɪʟʟ ʙᴇɴᴇꜰɪᴛ from adding informal modeling techniques to their repertoire. Since Ward Cunningham and Kent Beck wrote about them in their 1989 OOSPLA paper, CRC cards have been used by many. Brian Wilkerson, Laura Wiener, and I introduced CRC cards to a broader audience when we wrote about responsibility-driven design in *Designing Object-Oriented Software* (Prentice Hall) in 1990. In 1995, CRC cards are used extensively in teaching and when exploring early design ideas. CRC cards are an important modeling technique. Since CRC cards are informal, little has been written about their effective use. Instead, much has been communicated by word of mouth; people have earned their livelihood teaching and mentoring on CRC use. With this book, Nancy Wilkinson has advanced CRC card techniques. She describes how a hypothetical design team analyzes, designs, and thinks about objects. She carries us from analysis to implementation using CRC cards. This book is an important contribution to the lore and wisdom of CRC card use.

CRC cards embody a simple concept; they should be easy to use. Indeed, they have been readily adopted by many. Yet, some groups fail to use them successfully. There are several reasons why. In some cases, teams are simply struggling with understanding object concepts and design principles. In this book, Nancy takes us through the design of a sample library application; her book will give new designers plenty of direction and fodder for study.

Others find CRC cards too inflexible, too informal, or too limited. If you share these opinions, I urge you to reconsider them as you read this book. By their very nature, CRC cards aren't big enough to hold all your design and modeling ideas. They were never intended to tell the entire design story. Developers should be comfortable supplementing more formal design methods with CRC modeling sessions.

As Nancy points out, CRC cards can be a flexible tool that aids any group's object modeling activities. When cards are adapted to fit a group's methods and practices, they become an integral part of their design process. Over the years, I have collected stories about how people have modified CRC cards. Some have written implementation details, such as encapsulated state, on card backs. When cards are face up, this information is concealed, reinforcing the good design practice of hiding implementation details inside objects. I worked with a team that kept cards in a plastic box. The team leader passed out cards to members at the start of each modeling session. When computerized versions of CRC cards became available, they still preferred the informality of their design box.

I've worked with teams that kept lists of issues and lists of unassigned responsibilities. As they worked through design scenarios, these lists grew and shrank, and their CRC card decks expanded. Others have developed their model individually, then used CRC cards to walk a group through their design, keeping it at a fairly high level. Many have taped index cards to white boards, then drawn and redrawn message arrows between cards until they were satisfied. It was easy then to double check whether each card supported responsibilities used in an interaction sequence.

My colleagues and I have evolved our use of CRC cards. Today, backs of CRC cards are nearly as important as their faces; they are a place for recording seeds of ideas about our objects' roles, stereotypical behavior, and potential utility. Certain adaptations do not work as well as others. Replacing each card with an 8½" × 11" sheet of paper is not effective. It is much harder to assume the role of a big flimsy paper object. Instead, designers tend to fill up their paper objects with isolated details and ignore exploring different ways to divvy up responsibilities among objects.

Computerized CRC tools, while useful, do not replace interactive modeling sessions. There is something magical about waving cards in the air, grouping them in different ways to contrast their behaviors, or simulating a message send by shoving one card toward another. Computer tools often seem flat and lifeless by comparison.

Passing a rubber-banded deck of 200 cards off to a developer for implementation is unthinkable. Yet, some don't hesitate to hand off 200 pages of CASE-tool generated output, even if it is unintelligible. People need to communicate design intentions in a variety of ways; many of these ways will remain unsupported by even the cleverest tool vendor. Beware of using paper in lieu of face-to-face communications!

However, computerized design tools fill in where cards alone fall short. It is hard to share a CRC card design with a broad audience. Designs need to be recorded, communicated, and commented upon; on-line tools can greatly aid in this process. In her book, Nancy describes a process for using CRC cards. I encourage you to use them in the spirit in which they were created—an informal mechanism for developing and communicating object designs.

Rebecca J. Wirfs-Brock

Preface

The whole difference between construction and creation is exactly

this: that a thing constructed can only be loved after it is constructed;

but a thing created is loved before it exists.

— G. K. Chesterton, Preface to
Pickwick Papers, by Charles Dickens

$\mathcal{F}$OR THE PAST few years, several of my colleagues and I have been using CRC cards to help spread the use of object-oriented techniques throughout AT&T. I have conducted CRC card workshops to initiate software professionals into the world of object-oriented modeling. I have helped project teams use CRC cards for problem modeling brainstorm sessions to collect object data as input for their formal processes. And I have facilitated CRC card design sessions, using the cards to guide teams through object-oriented design. I have also helped some of these groups make the transition from CRC cards to C++.

When asked for CRC card references during these sessions, I pointed to various articles on the technique as well as to the chapters of some excellent books. But I never had any one book at my disposal that fully explained CRC cards and how they could be used throughout the product life cycle. Especially lacking was guidance regarding how the design on the cards could be best implemented in a C++ program. This lack of material did not seem strange to me at first, because I thought CRC cards were too simple a technique to warrant a whole book. But as I worked with more and more projects, I came to realize that practical information was needed about the CRC card process and how it contributes to object-oriented development at each stage of the software life cycle.

This book is the result of that realization, and the desire to codify my collective experience. I still think that CRC cards are too simple a technique to justify an epic volume (indeed, this is one of their biggest strengths). Therefore, I have tried to write a concise and manageable book which (like CRC cards) gets the point across without overwhelming the reader.

I believe this book will appeal to a wide audience, one that includes neophytes in object-oriented modeling who hope to use CRC cards to learn about objects; experienced object-oriented developers who want to learn how to use CRC cards to provide input to, or augment, their formal methodologies; and experienced software professionals who prefer informal techniques and want to understand how to use CRC cards at every stage of a project (in their design, in documenting a design that uses CRC cards, and in turning the design into C++ code). In essence, this book should be of interest to anyone who would like to participate in or facilitate a CRC card session.

Acknowledgments

W. Somerset Maugham once said, "There are three rules for writing.... Unfortunately, no one knows what they are." I learned that the most important rule is to have the support and encouragement of family and friends. I would also like to thank colleagues with whom I have shared sessions and numerous discussions about CRC cards, including Cecilia Castillo, Jim Coplien, George Logothetis, Dennis Mancl, Jim Rowland, and Gregg Vesonder. I would especially like to thank Gregg, my boss, for supporting my writing in spite of the effect it had on my "day" job. I am indebted to my editors, Peter Arnold, Richard Wiener, and especially Deirdre Griese, for guidance through my first foray into publishing. Deirdre's energy, patience, and humor have made it a much less painful process than it might otherwise have been.

I want to thank Rebecca Wirfs-Brock and Timothy Budd for giving me permission to share their words of wisdom in this book. This was especially meaningful to me because the books they wrote were the ones that sparked my initial interest in and understanding of objects and object-oriented design.

Thanks also go to my reviewers: Dave Annatone, Steve Bilow, Karen Brown, Liz Flanagan, Jim Rowland, Gregg Vesonder, and Richard Wiener. I owe special thanks to Liz for reviewing the earliest draft of the manuscript and putting up with my disappointment when she did not think it was perfect the very first time. Her many insightful comments, suggestions, and words of encouragement have helped to make this a far better book.

Contents

Using CRC Cards

Introduction

"Who cares for you?" said Alice ...

"You're nothing but a pack of cards!"

— Lewis Carroll
Alice's Adventures in Wonderland

EVERYBODY IS TALKING about objects. Presently, there are at least 27 published methods for doing object-oriented analysis and design. There are probably many more unpublished methods used by software development groups today[1]. Methodologies are extremely diverse and will continue to change for some time to come. Now is a time of confusion for anyone hoping to find *the* method for doing object-oriented development.

With all the hype surrounding particular object-oriented methods and notations, it is possible to miss the fact that there is an object-oriented way of thinking that must be mastered to effectively use this new technology. Project members may spend time and effort learning a particular method and tool and be no closer to understanding the essence of the object paradigm.

As the interest in object-oriented technology has grown in recent years, people have searched for ways to get their arms around the notion of objects and start object-oriented development while minimizing pain and risk. Class, Responsibility, Collaborator (CRC) cards provide a simple way for projects to investigate this new approach with minimal investment. Using simple index cards, CRC cards help convey, in an inexpensive, informal, and familiar way, an intuitive understanding of the object-oriented paradigm.

CRC cards have become popular not only as the initial step into the world of object-oriented technology, but also as support throughout the project life cycle. Projects that prefer informal approaches and those that are not yet ready to choose a formal method find CRC cards to be a convenient and natural way to develop a model of communicating objects.

This book is primarily aimed at small teams of people using CRC cards for all stages of the project life cycle. We have three main goals. The first is to convey the essence of the CRC card session: its informality, spontaneity, and energy, coupled with its power in creating an object-oriented decomposition of a problem. Readers interested only in an introduction to this simple technique may wish to read just the first 3 chapters. The second goal of the book is to describe the way CRC cards can support the analysis and design of a real object-oriented application. The third goal is to describe ways in which a design created with CRC cards can be effectively implemented in C++.

Roadmap

Here is what can be expected from the next 200 or so pages of this book. Chapter 1 is devoted to an overview of the object-oriented paradigm. It is not meant to be an exhaustive description of object-oriented technology, but it helps set the context for CRC cards. The aim is to promote a common understanding of the goal of the CRC card technique and to introduce terms that are used in the rest of the book. For a more complete description of objects and object modeling, the reader is referred to books by Booch[2], Wirfs-Brock[3], and Budd[4]. Readers experienced in object-oriented technology may wish to skim this chapter.

Chapter 2 introduces CRC cards and provides some history and motivation for the CRC card technique. We give credit to its inventors and early users and explore various areas where the cards have been used with success. This chapter also describes, at a high level, the role of CRC cards in a project life cycle. Finally, it presents the syntax of the card itself.

Chapter 3 describes the CRC card session in detail, including such topics as selecting a group, choosing a subset of the problem, brainstorming and filtering classes, choosing and walking through scenarios, handling potential pitfalls, and facilitating a CRC card session. This chapter attempts, through a simulated group session, to give the reader a feel for the interactions and issues in a real CRC card session. The example begun here continues through the next three chapters.

The remainder of the book is focused on the role of CRC cards in the project life cycle. Chapter 4 concentrates on their use for problem modeling. It describes the benefits and limitations of the process at this stage of the project. What distinguishes CRC cards for analysis in terms of classes, responsibilities, and scenarios is also explored. Finally, it describes the convergence to a stable problem model and what to do next. For groups that choose to use formal methodologies, CRC cards can help provide input to formal notations by bringing together the right people to brainstorm classes and behavior. The specific contribution of CRC card information to particular methods and notations is discussed.

Chapter 5 describes the use of CRC cards in the design phase. This includes a discussion of the strength and limitations of CRC cards for the design process. What distinguishes CRC cards for design in terms of classes, responsibilities, and scenarios is also explored. Enhancements to the cards are suggested that can facilitate their use in recording more detailed design information. This chapter continues the simulated group session into design. It also gives guidelines for documenting the cards and scenarios and tips for when prototyping should begin. Available tools for capturing a CRC card design are also described.

Prototyping C++ classes from a CRC card design is not a straightforward transliteration. Low-level design decisions must be used at this stage to bridge the gap between the cards and the code. Chapter 6 describes how CRC design elements map to C++ features and then how to build C++ classes using the CRC card input. This includes how the state of the objects are represented with C++ data members and how responsibilities, collaborations, and superclass/subclass relationships determine member function declarations and implementation.

Finally, the Appendix provides a listing of the class declarations and implementations for some key classes in the example application.

A Note on Programming Language

A number of languages support object-oriented programming, notably C++[5], Smalltalk[6], and Eiffel[7]. Although these languages have much in common, such as the direct support for object-oriented modeling concepts, they also differ in terms of philosophy and specific features. An application design will depend, to a great extent, on the choice of language. The target language that we have chosen and for which we can provide guidance is C++. The low-level design and implementation discussions in this book depend on C++ and do not pretend to apply to an implementation in any other language.

Common Terms

The following is a list of terms that are used throughout the book that may require some clarification or explanation.

Object-oriented model: We use this term to indicate either an object-oriented analysis or design, regardless of level of detail. It simply refers to a set of collaborating objects with accompanying scenarios.

Object-oriented development: This term will refer to all phases of software development: analysis, design and implementation, and testing, not just the implementation and testing stage.

Execution of scenarios: This term refers to the physical simulation, by a group of people in a CRC card session, of the steps and collaborations necessary to perform a system function. It does not refer to the execution of the program that implements the scenario.

Methodology: We define a methodology as a collection of disciplined processes used to generate models of a software system, using a well-defined notation. Many object-oriented methodologies exist today for projects that prefer formal methods. The CRC card technique is *not* a methodology.

Summing Up

CRC cards are a simple technique, but scrutinized closely, they prove to have much to offer. They are very good at helping to intuitively convey the idea of objects, and proper use of them will help a project model their application and translate their model into C++. My hope is that all of the above will also be true of this book.

Coming Up

We divert from the topic of CRC cards in Chapter 1 to provide an overview of object-oriented technology in general. This will help set the context for the CRC card discussions we return to in Chapter 2.

References

1. Jacobson, Ivar. "Time for a Cease-Fire in the Methods War." *Journal of Object-Oriented Programming* (July/August 1993), p.6 .

2. Booch, Grady. *Object-Oriented Analysis and Design with Applications,* 2nd ed. Benjamin-Cummings, Redwood City, CA, 1993.

3. Wirfs-Brock, Rebecca, Brian Wilkerson, and Laura Wiener. *Designing Object-Oriented Software.* Prentice Hall, Englewood Cliffs, NJ, 1990.

4. Budd, Timothy. *Introduction to Object-Oriented Programming,* Addison-Wesley, Reading, MA, 1990.

5. Ellis, M. A., and Bjarne Stroustrup. *The Annotated C++ Reference Manual,* Addison-Wesley, Reading, MA, 1990.

6. Goldberg, A., and D. Robson. *Smalltalk-80: The Language and Its Implementation.* Addison-Wesley, Reading, MA, 1983.

7. Meyer, B. *Object-Oriented Software Construction.* Prentice Hall, Englewood Cliffs, NJ, 1988.

CHAPTER 1

An O-Overview

"I think you are locating them in the wrong places. The

heart is on the left and the liver on the right."

"Yes, that was so in the old days. But we have changed all that."

—Molière, *le Médècin malgrè lui,*
act 2, scene 4

THE COMPLEXITY OF software problems and the high cost of their solutions has led to the continuous search for new approaches to software development. Certain of these new approaches take hold and, in time, become the de facto standard for the production of software. More than 20 years ago, structured programming, pioneered by E. W. Dijkstra[1], became the established way to solve software problems. Over the past decade, object-oriented programming has emerged. The object-oriented approach, with its potential for reusability and extensibility, has gained rapid acceptance in the software production community. While structured programming emphasized a hierarchical organization of problems by functionality, object-oriented programming organizes software around objects in the problem domain.

Developing object-oriented applications starts with finding these objects. But it also means understanding what knowledge and abilities are associated with each object and how they interact to get a job done. In this chapter we present a motorcycle tour of object-oriented development topics, such as the essential characteristics of objects and how they interact, the components of an object-oriented model, the object-oriented software development process, and object-oriented programming languages. The intent is not to teach these topics but to place the notion of CRC cards in the overall context of object-oriented development. We hope to motivate the use of CRC cards and illustrate how the notions of class, responsibility, and collaborator support object-oriented development.

The Object-Oriented Mind Shift

It has been said that conveying object-oriented techniques to a non–computer professional is easier than teaching them to someone who is experienced in procedural thinking, modeling, and programming. This is because the object-oriented way of decomposing a problem parallels the way non–computer professionals are used to looking at real-world situations. The decomposition is into entities that more closely resemble those in real-life situations. It makes sense that our software should model the problem we are solving as closely as possible. But most software developers have a view that has been formed by years of emphasizing the procedural aspects of the problem in order to mimic, and thus exploit, the linear processes of a computer.

In conventional software development, problems are decomposed by functionality, and the data structures that support the problem and solution are only loosely coupled with the behavior or procedures that operate upon them. In contrast, an object-oriented decomposition models a problem as the interaction of a set of entities whose data and behavior are inherent and inseparable. These entities, called objects, closely resemble those found in the problem domain. Typical examples of objects from various domains are instances of Menus, Employees, Chess Pieces, Lists, Books, and SpreadSheets.

What Is an Object?

Since objects are at the heart of this new approach, it is important to say explicitly what an object is. The best definition we have seen is the one coined by Smith and Tockey[2] and borrowed by Booch[3], which asserts that "an *object* represents an individual, identifiable item, unit, or entity, either real or abstract, with a well-defined role in the problem domain." An object is more than just data and functions bound together. It is a complete entity, either physical, such as an Employee or Chess Piece object, or conceptual, such as a Menu or a List object.

Objects, in software as in real life, are viewed as black boxes. They *encapsulate* information and behavior, restricting access to their internal parts and interacting with other objects in only well-defined ways. Essentially, an object has state, behavior, and identity.

State

Each object has a set of static properties, or attributes, which are its essential and distinctive characteristics. For example, Menu objects might have a list of option strings and a chosen option. Employee objects have names and salaries. SpreadSheet objects have cells.

The *state* of an object is the value of these attributes at any point in time. These may be simple values or the values of other objects. For example, a Menu object, called fileMenu, may have the value ("Close," "Open," "Save," "Print," "Exit") for its list of option strings and "Save" as the value of its chosen option, which represents its state. We can say that fileMenu "knows" the values of these attributes. A SpreadSheet object, called myBudget, will have a particular set of cells, each of whose value will be Cell objects, each with their own state. And an Employee object, called emp091037, might have a name attribute with value ("Nancy Wilkinson") and a salary attribute whose value is some small real number.

The state is private to the object and not directly visible to other objects. This concept of denying access to the internals of an object is called *information hiding*. The techniques of encapsulation and information hiding are not unique to an object-oriented approach[4]. But objects, and the direct support for these concepts in object-oriented languages, provide a particularly nice medium for their use.

Behavior

The behavior of an object is the set of operations, or *responsibilities*, it must fulfill for itself and for other objects. This includes the responsibility to provide and modify state information when asked by other objects as well as services to be performed at their request. For example, fileMenu may be responsible for displaying its options, collecting the chosen option from the user, and telling other objects the value of its chosen option when asked. Cell objects have the responsibility to display themselves or to update themselves when asked to do so by a SpreadSheet object.

Some of these responsibilities can also be hidden and used only by the object. The set of visible responsibilities form the *interface* of the object and completely define how it can act and react in relationship to other objects. The object has an integrity that cannot be violated; it is completely defined by its actions. It can only be modified, behave, or interact with other objects in very well-defined ways. An Employee object cannot display itself, a SpreadSheet object cannot provide salary information, and a Rook object simply cannot check out a library book or even move diagonally.

While an action may change an object's state, the values persist between invocations of its actions. A Queen's position, for instance, will be changed by its *move* operation, and the new value persists until it is modified by another operation. Therefore, the state of an object is dependent on the series of actions that the object has performed. For example, the value of a Cell object in a SpreadSheet depends on what update or edit operations have been done on it, and the position of a Pawn object on a Chess Board is the result of the set of moves it has made.

Identity

Each object is distinguished from all other objects by an *identity*, which is simply its inherent existence. A Person object with the name John will be different from all other objects of type Person with the same name. The Cell in row 4, column 5 of the SpreadSheet may have the same value as the Cell in row 6, column 2, but they are different objects with different identities.

Collaborators

An object cannot always carry out its responsibility on its own. It often needs the services

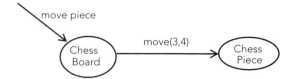

Figure 1.1 Sending a *move* message.

of another object. When a SpreadSheet objects asks a Cell object to display itself in order to fulfill its own *display* responsibility, it is collaborating with Cell, and Cell is said to be a *collaborator* of SpreadSheet. Asking a collaborator object to perform a service is done by *sending a message* to the object. The message consists of the responsibility name and any data that the collaborating object will need to perform the service.

For example, let's examine the operation of a chess program. Assume we have a Chess Board object to manage the interactions with the player and the Pieces on the board. In response to a message from the user to move a particular piece, the Chess Board object collaborates with the Chess Piece object via the *move* responsibility. This implies that Chess Board sends Chess Piece a message that consists of the responsibility name, *move*, and the data that represents the new position. This is illustrated in Figure 1.1. Ovals represent classes of objects, and collaborations are arrows labeled by the responsibility of the pointed-to class. The data (position) being passed is included in parentheses. Each object in an application has the set of attributes and behavior necessary to complete its portion of the activity of the system. Collaborations represent the way that objects work together to achieve the overall system behavior.

Class vs. Object

So far our examples have been talking about the "objects" that interact to solve problems. As we have said, objects represent the actual things in the problem domain that work together to accomplish a task. For example, fileMenu, myBudget, emp091037, and blackRook are all objects in various domains. Each object is an instance of a *class*, i.e., Menu, SpreadSheet, Employee, and Rook, which defines its essential characteristics and behavior. It is important to understand the distinction between class and object.

The class defines the structure and set of operations for all instances of that class, including how its objects are created. In the real world, there are entities, each of a particular type. In object-oriented modeling, these real-world entities are represented as objects, each of a particular class.

For example, the Menu class defines the structure of all Menus as a list of option strings and a chosen option. But many Menu objects can exist, each with different values for these attributes. The fileMenu object had specific values for its options strings and chosen option. Another Menu object, called editMenu, could have the list ("Undo," "Cut," "Copy," "Paste") as the value for its option strings, and any one of these strings may be the value of the chosen option at any point in time. All Menu objects have the same set of behaviors, such as displaying themselves and obtaining a choice from the user.

As another example, the Pawn class defines position as an attribute of all Pawns. But many Pawn objects (16 traditionally), each with their own position, participate in a game of chess. An object called blackPawn1 could have position (1,2), and another object called whitePawn8 could have position (8,7). All Pawn objects, however, have the same set of responsibilities, such as the ability to move in certain ways.

The Object-Oriented Model

Thus we have a set of objects, each an instance of some *class* that defines its state and behavior. Each has its own *responsibilities* and the knowledge and abilities to perform these tasks. An object *collaborates* with another when it needs a service from the object to fulfill one of its own responsibilities. This set of objects and a description of how the objects collaborate to fulfill the system behavior constitutes the *object-oriented model.*

I like to think of modeling a system with objects as being like organizing a set of individuals to solve a problem. Each has his or her own talents and strengths, and each is given a set of responsibilities that we trust them to carry out. They may need help from others to do this, but it is their business whom they ask for help and of what kind. We do not supervise every step, we simply put the right people together and start the ball rolling.

EXAMPLE **13**

Example

Next we will look at an example of an application and contrast a procedural decomposition with an equivalent object-oriented model. Consider an Electronic Checkbook application with the following system requirements:

> The electronic checkbook program is an application that supports a user's checkbook activities. The checkbook is a list of entries, each of a particular type. Users can record entries, e.g., checks, ATM withdrawals and deposits, payday deposits, in the checkbook. The checkbook program will calculate and record the new balance. The system will generate checks that correspond to check entries on request. The checkbook application will also search for and display particular entries or generate reports of sets of entries based on entry number, payee, tax status, or amount.

> For users who choose to receive their bank statements in disk form, the system will also balance their checkbook, automatically adding entries to the checkbook for transactions on the bank statement not accounted for in the checkbook.

If we were to decompose this problem in a structured, or algorithmic, way, we would have a set of procedures corresponding to the functions of the checkbook application, e.g., balance checkbook, add entry, search for entries. These procedures would be further decomposed into smaller procedures. For example, a procedural view of balancing a checkbook might look like Figure 1.2. In this procedural decomposition, we view the problem of balancing the checkbook as one process. It will be modular, but each module is simply a subprocess or a step in an overall process. The building blocks for this view are algorithms, e.g., clear checkbook entry, update working balance, that operate on data that are separate from the behavior. The rectangles in Figure 1.2 represent these processes. Solid lines represent sub-process relationships, and dotted lines represent potential data access by the processes.

In contrast, an object-oriented decomposition of the problem would contain important types of entities in this domain and the interactions of the objects that accomplish the processes of the system. Figure 1.3 contains a diagram of one possible object-oriented view of the problem. Checkbook objects have the overall responsibilities of the system that we listed before. The responsibilities of Bank Statement and Entry objects are called upon to help fulfill these overall responsibilities.

The building blocks in this view are the classes, and each class is assigned responsibilities that represent parts of the problem to solve, e.g., *search for entry* and *adjust balance*. Then objects of these classes collaborate to accomplish the task. Ovals in Figure 1.3 represent classes whose objects will collaborate to solve the problem. Thinner hollow-headed arrows represent patterns of collaborations, and labels on the lines represent

responsibilities of pointed-to classes. (Dark arrows represent superclass/subclass relationships, which will be discussed soon.)

The procedural approach differs from the object-oriented approach mainly in what
is viewed as building blocks for the model. But they also differ in their handling of the
data for the application. First examine the algorithmic decomposition of the problem.
The transient data used by the algorithms in this example can be local to the process, but
any persistent data, such as the checkbook or bank statement entries or balances, must
be global. This data is then potentially accessible to any of the processes. If its structure
changes, the entire system must be examined for potential updates.

On the other hand, consider the object-oriented decomposition. Because of the encapsulation and information hiding provided by objects, the persistent data used by the
application is within each object in its private state. Therefore, the data is only accessible

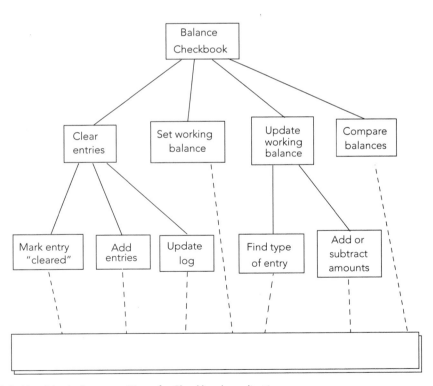

Figure 1.2 Algorithmic decomposition of a Checkbook application.

EXAMPLE   15

directly to the object itself. Other objects need to send messages to access this data. Any changes in the way data is handled or represented will require changes only to the state and behavior of one object.

For instance, suppose that for efficiency reasons the Bank Statement changes the way it stores its entries from a linked list to an array. This change implies that the way in which the Bank Statement performs its *know entries* responsibility will also have to be modified. Retrieval of entries will use array operations rather than list operations. But the change will be localized to Bank Statement and the way it fulfills its responsibilities. Checkbook will not interact with Bank Statement any differently than it did before. Thus, encapsulation and information hiding protects Bank Statement objects from unauthorized access by other objects, and it protects other objects from changes to the internal state of Bank Statement.

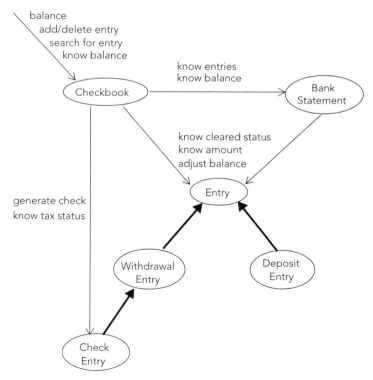

Figure 1.3 Object-oriented decomposition of a Checkbook application.

Let us emphasize that the procedural aspects of problems are still important, even in an object-oriented world. We must understand what the system does. The functionality of objects and the functionality provided by the interactions of objects are essential to the development of an object-oriented model. It could be said that in a procedural model, algorithms are used both for control and processing. But in an object-oriented model, algorithms are used only for processing.

Another difference between the object-oriented and algorithmic decomposition of a problem is that in a procedural model the data is artificially separated from the operations upon it. With the object-oriented approach, the data is reunited with the operations to form a more powerful modeling tool.

Superclass/Subclass Relationships

We also see in Figure 1.3 the representation of a class relationship that is very important to object-oriented systems. A *superclass/subclass relationship* exists between two classes when one class "is a kind of" the other class. In Figure 1.3, bolder solid-headed arrows between classes represent a superclass/subclass relationship, where the subclass is pointing at the superclass. For example, the subclasses Deposit Entry and Withdrawal Entry "are kinds of" Entrys. In turn, a Check Entry "is a kind of" Withdrawal Entry. Subclasses *inherit* the structure and behavior of their superclass. Therefore, common behavior and attributes can be defined once in the superclass rather than repeated in each subclass. All types of Entry (Withdrawal Entry, Deposit Entry, and Check Entry) objects know their amounts, cleared status, and other attributes, and all know how to report this information.

Certain behavior, although shared with the superclass, is carried out in a unique way by the subclass. For example, a Withdrawal Entry and a Deposit Entry will each have an *adjust balance* responsibility; but each will carry out this responsibility differently, in a way appropriate to its class. Other kinds of information and behavior are unique to and defined only in a subclass. For instance, a Check Entry has knowledge, such as tax status and check number, which it adds to the generic Withdrawal Entry knowledge that it inherits. It also has a *generate check* responsibility, which is not shared by its superclass.

A superclass may be abstract or concrete. An *abstract superclass* is created simply to hold information and behavior common to a set of classes. No object of an abstract superclass will ever be created in the application. For example, the Entry class defined here represents all knowledge and behavior common to Withdrawal Entrys and Deposit Entrys, but there will never be objects of type Entry. On the other hand, Withdrawal Entry serves as a *concrete superclass* for Check Entry, because there will be instances of the superclass in the application. In other words, there are Withdrawal Entry objects that are not Check Entry objects, such as ATM or other cash withdrawals.

Extensibility Through Polymorphism

Polymorphism (having many forms) is the ability of an entity in an object-oriented model to refer to objects of different classes at different times. How, and to what extent, polymorphism is supported in object-oriented languages varies. Polymorphism in a typed language such as C++ is constrained by the superclass/subclass relationship. An entity declared to refer to objects of a superclass can actually refer to objects of any of its subclasses at runtime. Thus requests sent to this entity will be carried out in a way appropriate to whichever subclass object is actually referenced at that time. The effect of this is that the behavior of a system written in terms of superclass objects can be extended simply by adding the definition of a new subclass.

For example, suppose that in the implementation of a chess game, we want to *display legal moves* for any piece chosen by the user. This behavior will be different for each type of piece. To display the legal moves of an arbitrary piece in a procedural model, we would test on the type of the Chess Piece (Queen, King, Pawn, etc.) and then execute the correct behavior for that type. Adding a new type of Chess Piece to the game would require defining *display legal moves* for the new type of Piece, then adding a branch to execute the new behavior for the new type wherever necessary.

An object-oriented implementation, on the other hand, will define a Chess Piece object that can actually refer to any kind of Chess Piece object chosen by the user. Simply sending a *display legal moves* message to that object will work correctly and in a way appropriate to that subclass. A new kind of Chess Piece, such as KnightRider (a piece that can make consecutive Knight moves) or a KnightMare (a piece that can move like a Knight or a Queen), can then be added to the system by defining it as a subclass of Chess Piece and redefining the *display legal moves* responsibility in a way unique to it (see Figure 1.4). All requests handled by Chess Piece objects will be handled appropriately by KnightRider or KnightMare objects with no change to the rest of the system[5].

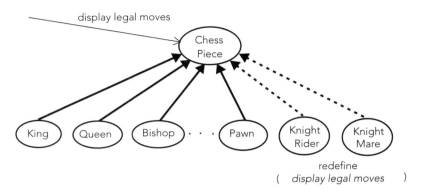

Figure 1.4 Defining new Chess Piece classes.

Scenarios

Notice that there is no explicit flow of control in Figure 1.3. The ordering of the responsibilities and collaborations can only be seen in an explanation of how the model accomplishes the system activities. *Scenarios* are specific examples of the use of the system. As we will see in Chapter 3, scenarios drive the development of an object-oriented model. And descriptions of how the model fulfills the scenarios are essential to understanding how an object-oriented system will operate.

For example, one scenario for the Checkbook application might be "What happens when a Checkbook balances itself?" Figure 1.5 is a subset of Figure 1.3 to which we will refer to help describe how the model fulfills this scenario. The following explanation is also necessary in order to explain the way in which a Checkbook object is balanced.

First, the Checkbook sets its working balance to the balance it gets from the Bank Statement object (via *know balance*). The Checkbook then asks the Bank Statement for each of its entries, using Bank Statement's *know entries* responsibility. It then either clears its own matching entry or adds the entry (via *add entry*) to its list. In order to clear an entry, Checkbook needs to collaborate with Entry, via *know cleared status*, to update its status to "cleared." Then the Checkbook object updates its working balance by collaborat-

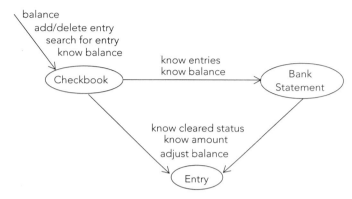

Figure 1.5 Scenario: A Checkbook object balances itself.

ing with each entry that is not "cleared." Each Entry knows how to *adjust balance* based on what type of Entry it is. Finally, Checkbook compares its real balance (via *know balance*) to its working balance and complains if they are not the same. This can also be depicted in a scenario table such as Table 1.1. We will discuss scenarios in more detail starting with Chapter 3.

Table 1.1 Scenario: Checkbook Balances Itself.

Client	Server	Responsibility	Comment
Checkbook	Bank Statement	know balance	set working balance to that of Bank Statement
Checkbook	Bank Statement	know entries	get each entry from BS
Checkbook	Checkbook	search for entry	find matching entry
Checkbook	Checkbook	add entry	if none, add new entry
Checkbook	Entry	know cleared status	otherwise, clear entry
Checkbook	Entry	adjust balance	update balance for each entry not cleared
Checkbook	Checkbook	know balance	compare balances

Object-Oriented Software Development

Developing software effectively using an object-oriented approach means abandoning not only the old way of viewing problems but also the old way of thinking about the software development process. The process still consists of the familiar three stages:

- *Analysis,* or problem modeling, in which the problem is described and represented

- *Design,* or solution modeling, in which a solution to the problem is discovered and represented

- *Implementation,* in which the code that makes up the working system is written and tested.

But the object-oriented approach allows, and in fact encourages, a more natural model of development than the traditional "waterfall" model of analysis *then* design *then* implementation. The encapsulation and information hiding provided by objects allows the development of highly modular abstractions, which interact only in well-defined ways. The relative independence of the objects encourages more incremental and iterative activities in the development process. Sets of objects can be analyzed, designed, and even prototyped before other parts of the system are fully analyzed.

This incremental approach to development has several advantages. First, it enables us to use what we learn from the prototyping of one part of an application in the design of another. Also, it encourages a much shorter interval between activity and feedback; that is, the customer can begin to see results in a shorter amount of time. Finally, if a system can be viewed as relatively independent parts, this approach strongly supports incremental (and more timely) deliveries of products or prototypes for user review.

The object-oriented software development process is best described as a process of iterative refinement. Each stage is revisited throughout the development process whenever a problem or inconsistency is uncovered. It is incremental and experimental, unashamedly backtracking to previous stages to change or complete the model. Analyze, design, develop, test, design, develop, analyze, design, develop, test is not an unknown pattern in the development of an object-oriented product.

We need to view the discovery of defects from previous stages as an expected and natural part of the process. Otherwise, we add hacks and workarounds to the implementation to cover defects rather than realign our design to handle new situations. The analyze-a-little, design-a-little, code-a-little cycle also improves upon the waterfall model because of its ability to accept feedback and rapidly respond to change. No one analyzes, designs, or builds an application right the first time. Encouraging iteration keeps the design intact and increases the understandability and maintainability of the resulting application.

Object-Oriented Programming

In order for a language to support object-oriented programming, it must provide a means for the implementation of the object-oriented concepts we have discussed. This implies that it should have features that directly support:

- Encapsulation and information hiding within classes

- Objects that are instances of classes

- Class inheritance

- Polymorphism

For example, C++ supports these object-oriented concepts in the following ways. In a C++ program, data and functions are encapsulated into abstract data types called *class*es, and objects that are instances of these class types can be created. Class *data members* represent the state, and *member functions* implement the behavior. The data members, as well as some of the member functions, can be hidden from other objects by declaring them to be *private* to the class. Member functions declared to be *public* form the interface of the class. Classes may be *derived* from other classes. Derived classes inherit data and functions from their *base* class. Polymorphism is supported in C++ by combining *inheritance* and *virtual functions.* Many of these features will be discussed more fully in Chapter 6.

   Although it is possible to translate an object-oriented model into a procedural-based program, the gains in terms of reusability and maintainability can only be achieved if the object-oriented concepts are carried through to the implementation. The development time will also be shorter and the mapping from design to code better maintained if the paradigm is consistent across stages.

Object Modeling: A Whole New Ball Game

Computer professionals are often so entrenched in their procedural world that it is difficult for them to make the mind shift to an object-oriented point of view. Alan Kay, for example, discovered that children learned Smalltalk faster than experienced programmers, who were blocked by their own preconceptions[6]. And Berard talks about "object blindness," the inability to identify objects or view a problem in an object-oriented way[7]. Because of this, it is often best to train people to think in objects by using a problem not usually associated with computers. We present such an example here to help the object-oriented initiate.

If you still think that you look at the world in a procedural way, think about the game of baseball. If you were to describe what happens in a baseball game to someone from a foreign country, would you describe it in a procedural or an object-oriented way? Put this book down and give it a try.

It is very difficult to model baseball in a procedural way. This is because what stands out in Baseball are the objects, e.g., Game, Team, Inning, Player. What each of these looks like and does is important, but the entities themselves are the most representative of the game. I have asked numerous people to describe the game to me. Each description I have received has reinforced my feeling that people see baseball, and most of the real world, in an object-oriented way. A succinct summary of these descriptions follows. As you read them, compare them to the way you view a baseball game. Think about how you would organize the classes and what an object-oriented model of the game would look like.

The most common descriptions of the game of baseball begin with a description of the structure of the Game and the Teams. A Baseball Game consists of nine innings in which 2 Teams, each with 9 Players, vie to score runs. Each Inning has 2 parts, in which one Team is batting and the other is fielding. Batting Teams try to score runs, and Fielding Teams try to stop them by getting outs. When the Fielding Team gets 3 outs, the half-inning is over and the Teams switch roles. The Team with the most runs at the end of 9 Innings wins.

Next, the responsibilities of each player are delineated. The Players on the Batting team sit on the bench and, one at a time, become Batters. The Batter has the responsibility to hit the ball into the Field and run to first base. If he succeeds and hits it where a Fielder cannot get it in time to get him out, he becomes a Runner. Runners have responsibilities such as running around the bases, tagging up, and stealing bases. If a Runner comes home, the Batting team scores a run.

Each Player on the Fielding Team, meanwhile, has the basic responsibility to field the ball hit by the Batter. If they do it by catching the ball before it hits the ground or throwing the ball to a base ahead of the Runner, the Runner is out. Some Fielders are Outfielders. They have the added responsibility to throw a fielded ball to a cut-off Player. Other Players are Infielders, and they have the added responsibility to cover bases and tag Runners. Basemen are Infielders who have responsibilities such as holding Runners on base. Pitchers are Infielders who have the responsibility to pitch the ball. Catchers are Infielders who have the responsibility to catch the pitched ball and throw out Runners trying to steal. Figure 1.6 shows the Player class hierarchy.

So far, the description of the game is a description of the entities, roles, and responsibilities of the Baseball domain. After this initial description of the Game, Teams, and Players, the person describing the game to me most often launches into scenarios. For example, if the Pitcher pitches 4 balls not in the strike zone, the Batter becomes a Runner at first base. If the batter hits the ball over the fence, it is a home run and he and all other Runners score runs. This is also when the interactions of the players become clear. If there is a Runner at first and the ball is hit to the Infielder called the Shortstop, who throws it to the Second Baseman, who covers second, and then the Second Baseman throws it to the First Baseman, who is covering first base, to get 2 outs. In general, base-

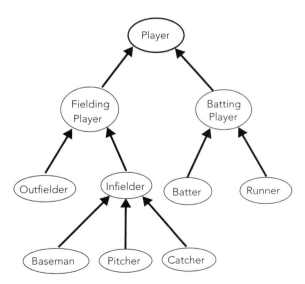

Figure 1.6 Baseball Player class hierarchy.

ball scenarios can be generated by following the ball. Descriptions of the different ways that the ball can be pitched, fielded, thrown, and caught provide an understanding of the workings of the game.

So the game of baseball is best described and understood as a description of the classes of entities of the game, the responsibilities of those classes, and scenarios that detail the interactions and collaborations of objects of those classes.

Summing Up

Moving from procedural development to object-oriented development means shifting from the old notions of process and data flows to thinking about problems in terms of classes, responsibilities, and collaborators. It means surrendering global control and learning to trust each object to carry out its tasks. Object-oriented modeling means finding these objects and understanding what knowledge, behavior, and relationships are associated with them. Making this shift can mean gains in maintainability and extensibility of the resulting application. But these gains are more likely to occur with accompanying changes in the software development process and the use of an object-oriented programming language.

Coming Up

In Chapter 2 and beyond, we will see how CRC cards support these fundamental notions of an object-oriented model and how the process that surrounds the cards helps to create such a model.

References

1. Dijkstra, E. W. "Notes on Structured Programming," in *Structured Programming*. Academic Press, New York, 1972, pp. 1–82.

2. Smith, M., and S. Tockey. *An Integrated Approach to Software Requirements Definition Using Objects.* Boeing Commercial Airplane Support Division, Seattle, WA, 1988.

3. Booch, Grady. *Object-Oriented Analysis and Design with Applications,* 2nd ed. Benjamin-Cummings, Redwood City, CA, 1993.

4. Parnas, David. "On the Criteria to Be Used in Decomposing Systems into Modules," *Communications of the ACM* 5(12):1053–1058 (1972).

5. Wilkinson, Nancy. "The Virtual Functions of C++." *UNIX REVIEW* 6(8):56–63 (1988).

6. Kay, Alan. "Microelectronics and the Personal Computer." *Scientific American* 237(3):230–244 (1977).

7. Berard, Edward. *Essays on Object-Oriented Software Engineering.* Prentice Hall, Englewood Cliffs, NJ, 1993.

CHAPTER
2

Introduction to CRC Cards

I opened the first pack of index cards and started making notes ... laying out the story as I understood it. I used this technique for every case I worked, pinning my cards on my bulletin board so that I could see how the story looked. ... The index cards permitted a variety of approaches: timetables, relationships, the known and the unknown, motives and speculations. ... At intervals, I took all the cards down and put them up again ... arranging them according to various schemes. What was I looking for? The link. The contradiction. Anything out of place. The known seen in a new light. The unknown rising to the surface.

— Sue Grafton[1]

$\mathcal{A}$ CRC CARD IS an index card that is annotated in a group setting to represent a class of objects, its behavior, and its interactions. CRC cards are created in informal brainstorming sessions, wherein functions of the application to be modeled are simulated and the outcome is recorded on the cards. The resulting set of cards describes an object-oriented model like the one we saw in Chapter 1 for the Checkbook application.

In this chapter, we will discuss the history and motivation for the CRC card technique, the ways in which the cards can contribute to the software development process, and finally the syntax of the cards themselves.

History of CRC Cards

CRC cards were introduced at OOPSLA in 1989 by Kent Beck and Ward Cunningham[2] as an approach for teaching object-oriented design. The technique was invented by Cunningham at Tektronix where he and colleagues, including Rebecca Wirfs-Brock and Brian Wilkerson, were struggling to help programmers move to the new paradigm. Cunningham believed that novices were hindered by trying to relate what they learned about objects to what they knew about procedural programming. In order to help students abandon the old way of thinking, he wanted to find, use, and teach fundamental concepts of object-oriented programming. The intention was to come up with the essential units of abstraction for the object-oriented approach analogous to the notions of processes, data flows, and data stores for procedural designs[3].

Cunningham arrived at *classes, responsibilities,* and *collaborators*[1] as the essential dimensions of an object-oriented model. He wrote the original CRC cards, describing the Hot-Draw drawing editor, early one morning after a sleepless night of pondering the problem. Characterizing objects along these 3 simple dimensions helped to deemphasize the details of a particular object-oriented language or environment and allowed programmers to concentrate only on the purely object issues.

The cards were first used by Cunningham with Dave Thomas in an object-oriented programming laboratory at Tektronix. Wirfs-Brock and Wilkerson, who also participated in this laboratory, later developed classes in object-oriented design based on their evolution of the technique. But CRC cards quickly spread outside of Tektronix and were popularized elsewhere by various proponents, most notably Kent Beck at Apple.

Cunningham spent some time implementing the CRC technique in an on-line tool using the Macintosh Hypercard system to support his personal work with a product team at Tektronix. However, he switched to the paper index cards for use in his class on object-oriented programming. Using index cards has some essential advantages over using a computer-based tool:

♦ They are portable. They can be used anywhere, away from any computers, even away from an office.

---

[1] Kent Beck, who wrote the first draft of their paper on CRC cards, changed the word *collaborator* to *helper*. Ward Cunningham, when he reviewed the paper, changed it back. CRC are the initials of Cunningham's son, who was born about that time[4].

♦ They are anthropomorphic. No computer tool could capture the essence of the interactions forced by the physical passing of the cards. Using index cards increased the level of involvement felt by each member of the team.

Useful tools have since been written to save a CRC card design on-line (see Chapter 5); but these tools serve only to record, enhance, and formalize the results of the brainstorming process, not to replace it.

Beck, Cunningham, Wirfs-Brock, Wilkerson, and others, such as Dave Thomas, Sam Adams, and Jim Coplien, have introduced thousands of novices to the object-oriented paradigm using index cards and these 3 dimensions. Sam Adams gained his early exposure to the technique at Tektronix before he left to form Knowledge Systems Corporation. KSC has been a major player in the acceptance of CRC cards.

Although Beck and Cunningham's emphasis was on introducing objects with CRC cards; others have emphasized their use throughout the software lifecycle. CRC cards are the basis of some work on building reusable software architectures[5]. They have also been used with much success as an approach for capturing object-oriented requirements[6]. Some members of the new Hillside Patterns Group, such as Beck, Cunningham, and Coplien, were pioneers of the CRC card technique. They see CRC cards as an excellent way to derive patterns for software design[7].

CRC cards form the basis for some more formal analysis and design methodologies. Rebecca Wirfs-Brock evolved her early work with CRC cards into the basis for the "preliminary design" phase of her responsibility-driven design methodology[8]. The Coad/Yourdon object-oriented analysis method includes a technique for finding objects called CardCase, which was influenced by Beck and Cunningham's work[9].

Use of the cards and the CRC technique have not been limited to software engineering. Coplien and Cain[10] have utilized the cards for capturing the essential aspects of organizational modeling. CRC cards are the basis for an environment that aids in understanding the flow of information in a development culture. Cards are used to describe Roles instead of classes; and the responsibilities define what the community can expect from a Role. Collaborations represent investment relationships between Roles.

CRC cards have become increasingly popular in recent years. As object-oriented technology has spread, so has the desire for a simple method to help computer professionals make the transition from process to object. And for many groups who enjoy an informal approach to software development, CRC cards can support their entire development cycle. As formal methods proliferate, CRC cards have become, for some projects, the simple low-risk alternative for doing object-oriented development.

CRC Cards in Software Development

The power of CRC cards for object-oriented development is in the group-based session that employs them. This session is described in detail in Chapter 3. This brainstorming process is used in multiple aspects and phases of the life of an object-oriented project. The basic framework for a typical project using CRC cards is a set of sessions whose emphasis moves gradually from analysis through design. A core group of people are participants in all the sessions, with the makeup of the group shifting from analysts to designers as the project moves through the life cycle. Throughout these sessions, participants learn in a very real way about object-oriented modeling. Sometimes it is also useful to run preliminary sessions to simply help the group make the paradigm shift without the pressure of building a useful model. The following discussion highlights the uses of CRC card sessions in the software development process.

Learning to Think in Objects

Despite the buzzing about object-oriented methods and tools, the true measure of how successful someone will be with objects is the degree to which he or she intuitively grasps the underlying idea of the object-oriented approach. Methodologies and tools cannot replace this gut-level understanding; they simply support the work done once the transition from process to object is made. Using CRC cards is an excellent way for people to begin to make this transition.

The use of the cards is familiar and requires learning a minimal amount before getting started. A well-run session is nonthreatening and fun. It is anthropomorphic, allowing students to get their hands dirty and become immersed in objects. Participants can't help but learn something. Use of the cards emphasizes the essence of object-oriented modeling: The separation of responsibilities and the fact that everything that happens is the result of an action of an object. In addition to introducing objects to willing participants, it is not uncommon for a CRC card session to convince sceptics that object-oriented modeling can work to solve a problem.

Analysis

The fact that the object-oriented approach more closely models the problem domain has been described as both the good news and bad news about objects. The good news is that if the domain is well understood, the solution is better able to support the workings of the application. The bad news is that it is more important than ever to understand the domain at all phases of the project. CRC cards and CRC card sessions are especially good at organizing and spreading domain knowledge at the analysis phase. Existing domain knowledge is shared in the sessions, and missing domain knowledge is identified. It is an effective, fun way for all participants to identify fairly high-level responsibilities and get a working problem model.

It is important to have the right objects modeling what the application will do before launching into sessions to determine how the objects accomplish their tasks. These design decisions will be made easier once a good working model of the application domain is built.

For some projects, CRC cards for analysis are a simple alternative to the myriad formal methods. Even for projects that will eventually use formal methods, the sessions and cards provide a way to promote an understanding of the problem domain and its object-oriented decomposition before jumping into a particular method and tool. The technique focuses on getting the right objects first, delaying the acquisition of details about how to produce the picture. (See Chapter 4 for more detail about the process that is used specifically for problem modeling.)

Design

CRC card design sessions build upon the model and momentum begun in the analysis sessions, refining responsibilities and bringing finer detail to the table. CRC card sessions provide a group environment for developing a solution model for the application. In design sessions, the responsibilities that represent what gets done in the application are broken down into lower-level responsibilities that represent a model for getting these responsibilities accomplished. Continuing CRC card sessions into design provides a consistent environment for development and facilitates the iteration that should exist between the analysis and design phases.

The informality and brainstorming nature of the sessions facilitate developing these solutions just as they facilitated the development of the problem model. The walkthroughs make the implementation concrete in specific instances. The role playing that takes place in the CRC card session is also useful for illustrating or explaining complicated designs to key personnel, such as new designers, developers, and testers. (See Chapter 5 for more details of CRC card sessions in the design phase.)

CRC Card Syntax

There is no universally accepted syntax for a CRC card. The only essential elements are the class name, a set of responsibilities, and a set of collaborators. Other issues, such as exactly how the collaborators are listed with respect to the responsibilities, whether or not to list attributes, and how to indicate subclass and superclass relationships, are up to the project using the cards. One of the strengths of the technique is its flexibility in this regard. Each person or project can customize the cards and the method in the way most useful to them.

The syntax illustrated in Figure 2.1 is the one we have found most useful in working with projects, especially projects using CRC cards from analysis through implementation. It reflects the Wirfs-Brock evolution of the Beck and Cunningham CRC cards, making them more accommodating for design and more useful as a blueprint of a C++ program.

The card shown in Figure 2.1 is a 4″ × 6″ lined index card. 3″ × 5″ cards are often used for analysis; but a 4″ × 6″ card allows you to write larger and handles the more detailed responsibilities that are listed in the CRC card sessions of the design phase.

The class name is written on the top of the card. Class names form a vocabulary for the CRC card discussion. For example, Checkbook, Entry, and Bank Statement are classes in the Checkbook domain, and Player, Catcher, and Batting Player are class names in the Baseball domain. Well-chosen names can greatly increase the understand-

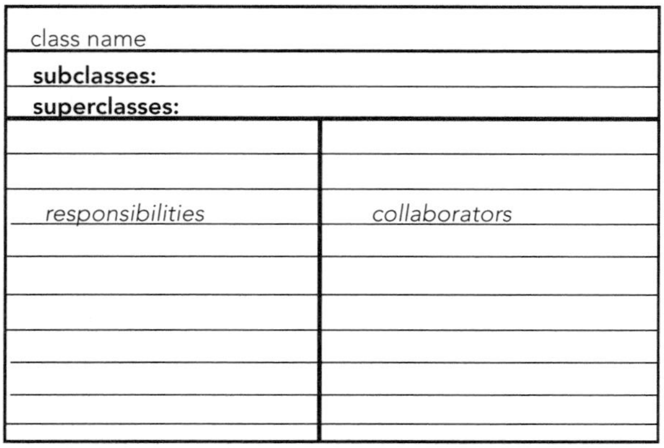

class name	
subclasses:	
superclasses:	
responsibilities	*collaborators*

Figure 2.1 Suggested format for a CRC card.

ability of the model. The names chosen here for the class will probably be used for years by people involved in continued analysis, design, and implementation as well as testing and maintenance.

The next two lines of the card are reserved for listing superclasses and subclasses, if they exist. For example, the Withdrawal Entry card for the checkbook application will list Entry on its superclass line and Check Entry on its subclass line.

The rest of the card is divided into two columns. Responsibilities of the class are listed on the left. Responsibilities are the knowledge that a class maintains and the services that it provides. For example, *know balance* and *search for entries* are responsibilities of a Checkbook class, and *pitch* and *strike* are responsibilities of a Pitcher class. Responsibility names should be concise but descriptive, and they should always contain an active verb.

The collaborators for the responsibilities are listed on the right of the card. A collaborator is a class whose services are needed to fulfill the responsibility. For example, a Checkbook collaborates with Bank Statement objects to fulfill its *balance* responsibility. A Pitcher will need to collaborate with a Catcher in order to *pitch.*

The collaborators are listed directly across from the responsibilities that they help to fulfill. This implies that the responsibility/collaborator relationship is one-to-many—there may be many collaborators to fulfill one responsibility—and that collaborators may be listed more than once on a card if they are helping to fulfill different responsibilities. For example, Checkbook needs to collaborate with Entry for both the *search for entries* and the *balance* responsibilities. Therefore, Entry will be listed twice in the collaborator column of the Checkbook card, across from each of these responsibilities.

There are three important things to know about collaborations when using CRC cards. First, collaborations exist *only* to fulfill responsibilities. The existence of a collaboration implies that there is a responsibility of the collaborator class, which is needed by the class initiating the collaboration. One possible extension to the syntax of the CRC card (especially useful for design) is to note this collaborating responsibility on the card next to the collaborator (see Chapter 5).

Second, collaborations will only be listed when one object actually sends a message to its collaborator. In general, we do not use collaborations to fulfill responsibilities to know or maintain information unless that knowing or maintaining requires some interaction with another class.

Finally, collaborations are modeled as a one-way communication from the initiator class to the collaborator. The collaborator class is assumed to perform the requested service or return information as part of the original request, rather than as a separate collaboration.

What you cannot see in Figure 2.1 is a list of attributes on the back of the card. This is appropriate since the focus of the CRC card technique is the *behavior* of the object, not the structure. But sometimes people like to think about what an object has at the same time or even before they think about what it does. Participants modeling a Checkbook class, for example, may like to capture the fact that it *has* a collection of Entrys first, and think about the behavior (maintaining or *know*ing its Entrys) later during scenario execution. It is useful to have a place to record these attributes if they are helpful.

It is also important to have a succinct definition for the abstraction represented by the class. This can also be entered on the back of the card. Formulating this definition may seem the most tedious part of the exercise, but it is also one of the most critical. Agreeing early about the abstractions can avoid problems later.

Figure 2.2 shows CRC cards (front and back) describing the Checkbook and Check Entry classes from the Checkbook application of Chapter 1.

Why CRC Cards?

Why have CRC cards proven to be a useful and popular technique for introducing the object-oriented paradigm and for doing object-oriented modeling? The biggest contributing factor to the success of CRC cards is the fact that the cards and the exercise are nonthreatening and informal, providing a good environment for working and learning.

Because the methodology is so simple, it does not overwhelm the task of developing an object-oriented model, and the group interactions foster a creativeness in the participants that facilitates the brainstorming of good solutions. The CRC card session gets the right people into the room and engages participants in dialog that uncovers the needs of the system.

Another advantage to the technique is the concrete role that the index cards play in the simulation of an application. The physical nature of the cards emphasizes the division of responsibility across objects. It also encourages an intuitive understanding of the model. When someone holds a card, saying "I need to do this," and points at someone else, saying "I need you to do that," they experience the design firsthand in a way that is impossible to produce using textual representations.

Also, the size of the cards provides a guideline for class complexity. If you need more than one card, then it may be time to examine the class. Can the responsibilities be phrased more succinctly? Does the class have too much responsibility? Should it delegate more? It is certainly possible for a class to be more complex than a single card, but the size is a warning flag to take a look at the emerging model.

Checkbook: the object in the system that maintains users' checkbook entries and balances the checkbook

Checkbook	
balance	Bank Statement, Entry
add/delete Entry	
search for Entry	Entry
know balance	

Check Entry: The set of objects that represent entries in the checkbook that correspond to written checks

Check Entry	
superclass: Withdrawal Entry	
know check number	
know tax status	
generate check	*Print Subsystem*

Figure 2.2 Sample CRC cards from the Checkbook application.

Other advantages are that the cards are inexpensive, portable, flexible, and readily available. This advantage may work against them at times. Kent Beck has been quoted as saying that some people do not trust a tool that only costs a dollar. Many people, however, see this low-tech, inexpensive approach as a low-risk way to investigate object-oriented techniques and a low-overhead way to build an object-oriented application.

Because the cards are cheap, made of paper, and easily created, they do not feel as permanent as designs entered into a computer. They can be freely added to or ripped up to rapidly revise designs and evaluate different approaches. This supports the iterative nature of object-oriented design and the essential part experimentation plays in all nontrivial software development.

But the most remarkable thing about CRC cards is that, despite their simplicity and flexibility, they actually capture the essential aspects of the design: classes, responsibilities, and the patterns of interactions of the objects of these classes. Because of this, they are not just a simple technique for introducing objects. They can be, and are, used effectively for real software development.

Why Index Cards?

The question often comes up: what is so special about index cards? Couldn't we use Post-its® or flip-charts or notebook paper? The answer, of course, is yes.

As with many aspects of the CRC card technique, a project should choose a physical medium that facilitates its own process and understanding. The essential element, the esprit de corps, of the CRC card process is the interaction, the brainstorming, the sharing of knowledge and the way the physical representation of classes stresses the separation of responsibilities, encourages the exploration of multiple designs, and requires the full participation of those involved. That being said, I'd like to put a plug in for sticking with old-fashioned index cards.

Index cards have some advantages over the alternatives we have used. Post-its are nice because they stick to walls, but so do index cards with magnets and a white board. Because of their stickiness, looking through a pile of Post-its for a specific class is less than optimal. Post-its also are less robust than index cards and do not have lines. This makes the lining up of collaborators with responsibilities more difficult. And if you like to write attributes and definitions on the back, watch out for the glue on the Post-its.

The other medium we have used in a session was flip-chart pages pinned to the wall. This has the advantage of allowing everyone in the room to more easily see the classes, but the vision problem would have been more profitably solved by decreasing the number of people in the room. Hanging the "cards" on the wall discouraged lively execution of scenarios and the feeling of ownership of the classes. The sheets were not lined, and we needed an extra one to represent the back of the card. No one volunteered to collect the "cards" at the end of the day and enter them into their on-line CRC card tool. The sheets were just too hard to work with.

Index cards are a familiar tool for this kind of job. How many of us were taught in school to use index cards to hold tidbits that would eventually come together to form our term paper? Even my reference book for doing a bibliography suggested the use of index cards to hold the names of books. I still use index cards to store information about dishes I will (someday) prepare. Finally, I found in my *Manuscript Development Guidelines* a helpful hint suggesting the use of cards to create an index for this book.

Does this discussion seem silly? To some extent it is, but it is amazing how people form opinions of the best medium to use after just a few rounds of a CRC card session. Whichever medium a project chooses, it should be familiar, comfortable, and easy to work with so that it doesn't add extra work to the modeling or design task at hand.

A Note on the Flexibility of the Technique

The informality and flexibility of CRC cards and the process that surrounds them is one of the major strengths of the technique. The customizability of the process and medium is an enormous advantage of the cards. However, the lack of formal structure can be disconcerting for someone new to object-oriented technology.

For example, the syntax of the cards in terms of fields to be included and placement of the entries can be different for different projects. But newcomers to the method like to follow a model when making up each of their cards. We introduce a specific syntax for a CRC card in order to provide such a model and to emphasize what we have found to be the important aspects of CRC cards.

By adding some guidelines initially, a group can use the cards in a standard way to become comfortable with the process and the object model. Once the members are more knowledgeable, a group can decide how to use CRC cards to support their own notions and understandings. At that point, the flexibility and customizability becomes an enormous advantage of the CRC card technique. Throughout the book, we will point out where projects have choices in using the cards or structuring the process. But we will always give guidelines and suggestions for which choices we have found to be most useful so that people new to the world of object-oriented technology and CRC cards have a starting point from which to work.

Summing Up

CRC cards were created by Ward Cunningham at Tektronix to help students learn the essentials of object-oriented programming. He, Kent Beck, and others have initiated thousands of computer professionals into object-oriented technology using index cards and classes, responsibilities, and collaborators. Since then, CRC cards have been used by many projects doing real object-oriented development to support their development process.

Coming Up

In Chapter 3, we explore how the cards we have introduced here are used in interactive sessions to develop a problem model for an example application. Guidelines for setting up a session, using the cards in the session, and facilitating a session are also discussed.

References

1. Grafton, Sue. *"I" is for Innocent,* Henry Holt and Company, New York, 1992, pp. 236–237.
2. Beck, Kent, and Ward Cunningham. "A Laboratory for Teaching Object-Oriented Thinking." *OOPSLA-89 Proceedings, SIGPLAN Notices* 24 (10):1–6 (October 1989).
3. DeMarco, Tony. *Structured Analysis and System Specification.* Yourdon Press, Englewood Cliffs, NJ, 1978.
4. Beck, Kent. "CRC: Finding Objects the Easy Way." *Object Magazine* 3(4):42–44 (November/December 1993).

5. Buschmann, Frank. "Rational architectures for object-oriented software systems." *Journal of Object-Oriented Programming* 6(5):30–37 (September 1993).

6. Kamath, Yogeesh H., Ruth E. Smilan, and Jean G. Smith. "Reaping Benefits with Object-Oriented Technology." *AT&T Technical Journal* 72(5):14–24 (September/October 1993).

7. Coplien, James. "Software Designs: The Emerging Patterns." *C++ Report* 18–22, 66–67 (July/August 1994).

8. Wirfs-Brock, Rebecca, Brian Wilkerson, and Laura Wiener. *Designing Object-Oriented Software.* Prentice Hall, Englewood Cliffs, NJ, 1990.

9. Coad, Peter, and Edward Yourdon, *Object-Oriented Analysis,* 2nd ed. Yourdon Press, Englewood Cliffs, NJ, 1991.

10. Coplien, James. "Examining the Software Development Process." *Dr. Dobb's Journal* 19(11):88–95 (February 1993).

CHAPTER
3

The CRC Card Session

The play's the thing . . .

— William Shakespeare,
Hamlet, act 2, scene 2

THE MOST IMPORTANT aspect of the CRC card technique is not the cards themselves, but the creation of the cards in interactive sessions. Groups of people responsible for modeling and solving the problem gather in a room and use the cards to guide the choice of classes, responsibilities, and collaborators. The nonthreatening and creative nature of the sessions facilitate finding the best classes and investigating scenarios to the fullest. And the anthropomorphic and informal approach used in a group setting encourages participation and helps members of the group become experienced users of the object-oriented paradigm.

Chapter 2 described the role of CRC card sessions in various stages of a project life cycle. This discussion differentiated the problem-modeling and solution-modeling phases. Chapters 4 and 5 will highlight the aspects of the process and cards that are unique to each of these stages. Our focus is on small teams who will use CRC card sessions to do analysis and design, and much of what we describe is common to both stages. The example in this chapter describes the CRC card session for a new application; thus, the emphasis is more on modeling the problem than designing the solution. The design aspects of the application modeled here will be discussed in Chapter 5.

Getting Started

In this section we discuss issues that influence a CRC card session but that precede the session itself.

Choosing the Group

A key activity preceding a CRC card session is the selection of the group of participants. Rather than issuing an open invitation to anyone interested in objects or the problem to be modeled, the selection of the group should be carefully made from the set of people involved in the project. Certain characteristics of a group increase the chance of a productive CRC card session. These characteristics can be divided into three categories: size, participants, and group dynamics.

GROUP SIZE

The optimal size for a CRC card problem-modeling session seems to be five or six participants. If there are more than six people in a session, the number of real or perceived differences in viewpoints and opinions become a liability. Also, members of large groups are prone to side conversations resulting in the loss of a common base of information. The number of disagreements increases and is almost exclusively the result of communication issues rather than technical issues. Figure 3.1 provides a visual image of how quickly the potential paths of communication (and miscommunication) increases as the number

Figure 3.1 Potential patterns of interaction with four, five, and eight participants.

of participants grows. Another problem with too large a session is that groups of cards that should logically belong to one person may be artificially split simply to ensure that everybody owns a card.

In a group of five or six people, generally everyone can productively participate. And the different viewpoints, biases, or outlooks are an advantage rather than a liability. They contribute greatly to the formulation of a good problem model. A group smaller than five, however, may not have the necessary range of problem domain and solution domain expertise. After the problem is modeled, subsequent design sessions modeling the solution may require fewer people, although three or more members seems necessary for the formulation of a good design.

A project may have more people beyond the core group who want to learn about objects or who want to understand the problem model or design of an application. One solution for these projects is to allow the extra people to be present strictly as observers to the process. Another possibility is to run small workshops for these people in which the model is exercised and explained.

GROUP PARTICIPANTS

Who should be in this group of five or six? People who embody the domain knowledge and object-oriented experience need to be present. The people who are responsible for turning the problem model into a working system should also participate in the CRC card sessions from the beginning in order to learn the domain as early as possible. Also, design influence early on can help build a problem model that maps more directly to design and implementation.

As the sessions move from problem modeling into design, the percentage of domain experts can decrease, but at least one domain expert should remain to validate design choices relating to the problem domain. Design sessions may also include testing personnel to help them understand how the system is supposed to operate.

DOMAIN EXPERT

In the early sessions, the most important contribution comes from the domain expert. The domain expert understands what the system should do and probably knows very little about how it can be accomplished. This keeps his or her perceptions about what needs to happen free of biases based on what is hard, possible, or fun to implement. The domain expertise is what feeds the process of problem modeling by helping to create the scenarios and to choose the classes based on problem-related abstractions. At least one domain expert should be present in a modeling group. If the author of the requirements document is not the domain expert, then he or she should also be present to discover and clarify inevitable ambiguities.

OBJECT-ORIENTED TECHNOLOGY FACILITATOR

Object-oriented expertise is a large contributing factor in the success of a session. This expertise may come from an outside facilitator or from a member of the group who takes on the facilitator role because he or she is more experienced than others in the object-oriented approach. There are several advantages to an outside facilitator. First, it is easier for an outsider to encourage all team members to participate regardless of previous group dynamics. Also, having an outsider assume this role frees the object-oriented experts on staff to participate and not be burdened with the added responsibility of facilitating. An outside facilitator is generally domain ignorant and can sometimes produce surprisingly insightful questions. He or she can serve as a catalyst or an objective observer, asking good questions about the application. Such questions or comments are free of the biases, assumptions, and preconceived notions held by the other members of the team.

Whether or not the facilitator is a member of the project team, the object-oriented expert can aid the CRC card analysis and design process by guiding the formulation of abstractions. The chance of choosing good classes with meaningful names and a minimal but sufficient set of responsibilities can be increased by someone knowledgeable in object-oriented design techniques.

For groups largely new to object-oriented modeling, the most important reason to have a person knowledgeable in object-oriented techniques present in the group is so that their expertise can be spread throughout the group in a transfer of knowledge by example. For these groups, this transfer of knowledge should be the main goal of the facilitator. (See *Facilitating a CRC Card Session* at the end of this chapter for more information on this topic.)

MANAGERS

Whether or not to encourage, or even allow, managers to participate in a CRC card session is an interesting issue. The managers' "need to know" must be balanced against the impact of their presence on the session dynamics.

Managers should be knowledgeable enough about CRC cards and object-oriented software development in general to feel comfortable with the iteration in the process and the seeming chaos of the sessions. Managers who do not understand the object-oriented approach well enough to support a software development process of iterative refinement will not be able to provide an environment where an object-oriented project can thrive[1].

Sitting in on a facilitated session can help managers see the process, and the progress, firsthand. Watching a session facilitated by an expert ensures that managers understand the CRC card activity and, at a high level, the fundamentals of object-oriented modeling. It has also proven to be a good way to sensitize managers to technical, sociological, and staffing issues that come into play in object-oriented development[2].

Unfortunately, managers can inhibit, or even halt, the process. Even when the manager trusts the staff and supports the use of object-oriented techniques, his or her presence in a working session is a detriment. Project members do not want their manager sitting next to them looking over their shoulder when they work.

To familiarize managers with the process without hindering the progress of the group, special introductory sessions can be run for managers. The focus of the session can be on the project they are managing. The session should be long enough to provide a learning vehicle without doing full-scale modeling for project development. Such an introduction gives managers a feel for the process and the object-oriented point of view. They can then leave their staff to do the actually modeling and design in working sessions.

GROUP DYNAMICS

Group or project dynamics is an important factor in the success or failure of a CRC card session. The best CRC card sessions bring together groups of people who have common goals and agendas, work well together, respect each other, and are not dominated by one or a few of the members. While this may sound like an ideal, many projects come close enough to this description to have a good working session devoid of personnel issues. Newly formed project teams, who come into CRC sessions with somewhat more diverse interests, fears, and goals, sometimes find that the interactions are a unifying experience.

The interactions can improve intragroup relationships by getting everyone's abilities, knowledge, biases, and interests out on the table.

Some projects, whose project team members do not agree and communicate poorly, plan a CRC card session in hopes of mending fences through this team-building experience. These sessions are doomed to failure. CRC card sessions, while relying on good group dynamics for success, are technical activities. They can improve interactions by giving everyone a forum for airing and hearing viewpoints and concerns relating to the problem, but they do not work miracles in cementing relationships. A group must have the potential for a reasonable working relationship at the start of the sessions. As Bjarne Stroustrup has said, "Don't try technological fixes for sociological problems"[3].

Another potentially destructive situation in a CRC card session is the presence of a participant who dominates the group and will not compromise. If there is one person whose goals or sensitivities clearly diverge from those of the group, the other members can sometimes convert (or, in the worst case, ignore) the outlier. But if that person has a position of power in the group (political, organizational, or emotional), he or she can sabotage an entire session.

To summarize, when choosing the participants for a CRC card session, select about 5 or 6 team members who encompass the necessary domain expertise, design expertise, and object-oriented expertise. The people chosen should form a group that has a unified set of goals and that can potentially work well together.

Preparing for a Session

Some preparation on the part of the participating group is necessary before embarking on a set of CRC card sessions. The most important input to the process is a requirements document. This document can be at varying levels of detail and formality, but it should include a problem statement with associated goals for the application, a description of the operation of the system, and a set of constraints. This document may be augmented or corrected as a result of a CRC card session, but the core of this information is necessary to start. Generally, a project that cannot provide this information is not ready to begin modeling.

Certainly, everyone should have read and familiarized themselves with any of the documentation that will be used in the session. But it is also best if the group does some reading on object-oriented techniques and CRC cards. It is particularly helpful if they have participated in a CRC card session to learn about objects before beginning their problem-modeling sessions.

Choosing a Subset of the Problem

It is essential when running a CRC card session to have the focus be on one fairly small and manageable portion of the system at a time. If the set of classes and functionality being modeled is too numerous, diverse, or open-ended, a large part of the session can be spent writing classes on cards whose number and contents never converge. This makes the session frustrating and does not provide a good environment for learning about the object-oriented approach.

The partitioning of a problem into subsystems is not done simply in preparation for a CRC card session. This high-level partitioning of the domain is important in every object-oriented development project. An object-oriented system can be seen as a set of subsystems, each a cluster of highly connected classes that interact to perform a portion of the system functionality. These subsystems then interface in well-defined ways, usually through objects of an interface class. Object-oriented analysis and design is best done one subsystem at a time.

Subsystems can sometimes be inferred from the requirements. If not, a high-level functional partitioning of the system can be done as a starting point for the modeling. A subdivision based on system function will still limit the problem effectively for use in the session.

The Session

The CRC card session is a fast-paced, creative exchange. Classes are discovered, converted into cards, and then annotated with responsibilities and collaborators through the physical simulation of the system. Each person is responsible for holding, moving, and annotating one or more cards as messages fly around the system in support of a particular need or activity. Participants create, supplement, stack, and sometimes even wave cards as they "become" the objects during the walk-throughs of the scenarios. And to almost everyone's surprise, a model of communicating objects slowly begins to emerge.

This section describes the CRC card session itself. General guidelines and rules of thumb for the mechanics of a session are interspersed with examples of their use for modeling a simple system. The example provides additional heuristics and a feel for the interactions of the group members in a typical session.

The Problem

In the sample session presented here, the participants will be modeling a library system for checking out, returning, and searching for books. The requirements for the system are as follows:

> This application will support the operations of a technical library for an R&D organization. This includes the searching for and lending of technical library materials, including books, videos, and technical journals. Users will enter their company ids in order to use the system; and they will enter material ID numbers when checking out and returning items.
>
> Each borrower can be lent up to five items. Each type of library item can be lent for a different period of time (books 4 weeks, journals 2 weeks, videos 1 week). If returned after their due date, the library user's organization will be charged a fine, based on the type of item (books $1/day, journals $3/day, videos $5/day).
>
> Materials will be lent to employees with no overdue lendables, fewer than five articles out, and total fines less than $100.
>
> … (Design Constraints) …

Participating in the session are two library domain experts: Betty, who wrote the system requirements, and Dewey, a librarian, whose work will be off-loaded by the system. Both Dewey and Betty have been involved in building other library applications. Two designers and implementors, Cecilia and Jim, who know something about library systems are present. The session is being facilitated by Nancy, an object-oriented expert who initially knows little about library applications.

The group makes a decision to leave the functions of the user-interface subsystem and database subsystem until later. No subsystems beyond these are evident from the requirements. But the group decides to partition the problem functionally and to concentrate first on the daily operations of the library such as checking out, returning, and searching for books, journals, and videos. Later they can analyze how to add other system functions, such as generating overdue notices and sending bills to users' organizations.

Creating Classes

The first step in modeling an object-oriented system, and thus the first step in the CRC card process, is finding classes in the problem domain. Classes can be listed with the entire group in a first step before creating any cards. Alternatively, classes can be encountered and created as part of the execution of the scenarios. Different groups may find different methods useful.

Starting a group off by brainstorming classes together emphasizes that this is a group effort, and it gives everyone a chance to get involved in the process from the beginning. It seems to be a nonthreatening way to introduce a group to a new situation and new technology. In addition, it provides a framework of classes, however preliminary (a house of cards?), upon which to begin distributing responsibilities during the walk-through of the scenarios. New classes will certainly be discovered during scenario execution, but the major classes can usually be identified at this early stage.

BRAINSTORMING

The brainstorming process consists of one person standing at a board writing names of classes as they are suggested by the session participants. At this stage, not much discussion is tolerated about whether or not the abstraction will turn out to be a "real" class. More experienced groups can filter at the same time as classes are suggested, but in newer groups, criticism of proposed classes can cause team members to withdraw from further participation. A separate filtering stage can take place after the brainstorming in which the classes are examined. Obvious redundancies are removed then, and sometimes names are changed. More subtle redundancies and changes in the class structure may also need to take place later while walking through scenarios.

Where do the names of the classes come from? The main source of class names will be the people involved in the project and the CRC card session. People who know their application can usually come up with a fairly complete set of classes, at least at the analysis stage of the process. The concepts that describe *what* the system should do are readily available to the domain experts in the room. At this stage we discover the key abstractions in the problem domain. Later, in design, we will create additional classes to support the solution of the problem.

Classes can be derived from reading the requirements document and looking for the major concepts, but the domain experts provide the filter for the concepts in the requirements document. Scanning the document is a good mechanism to jog the memory of participants should they get stuck. This practice also ensures that all known requirements are considered when looking for classes.

It may happen that the object-oriented facilitator needs to ask some pertinent questions or suggest some common types of classes to get a shy, or stuck, group going. Should we model physical objects? How about interfaces to other parts of the system? Can the name of the application suggest classes? Classes may represent tangible or visible things, roles, events, or concepts.

In the Library CRC card session, Nancy stands at the board soliciting classes while Dewey, Betty, Jim, and Cecilia offer suggestions. The group brainstorms the following set of classes: Library, Librarian, User, Borrower, Article, Material, Item, Due Date, Fine, Lendable, Book, Video, and Journal. At one point Jim wonders whether the User class is actually outside the scope of the system, and Cecilia questions whether Library and Librarian overlap too much to be separate classes. Nancy reminds both of them that anything goes during brainstorming and that they will deal with those issues next.

FILTERING CLASSES

As the number of classes being suggested decreases, the session gradually enters a filtering stage, wherein classes are examined more closely. During this stage, we use the requirements plus the knowledge of the people in the room to eliminate redundancies, identify missing abstractions, and recognize related classes.

An important activity of this stage is to discuss and agree upon short, precise meanings for the abstractions. These will be entered on the back of the cards. For example, the Book class could be defined as *the set of objects that represent books to be borrowed from a library.* Everybody in the room should understand precisely what is meant by each class. This can take some time in the beginning, but it saves time and avoids misunderstanding later on. This definition can only be achieved if some participant in the session has a good understanding of the concepts of an application. If no one in the room understands what a suggested class really is, someone else should be brought into the room. This public definition process also ensures that everyone else in the room acquires necessary domain understanding.

As we examine the preliminary list of classes for the Library system, the participants have many questions and comments. Jim wonders again whether the actual Library User is outside the scope of the model being created here. Nancy suggests that they keep User as a class. If after executing scenarios the class has no responsibilities, then it can be discarded. There is nothing lost by keeping the card on the table in the meantime. Cecilia next brings up her question about the difference between Library and Librarian. This requires more discussion and the formulation of a definition for each.

Nancy asks who suggested the Library class. When Dewey raises his hand, Nancy asks him exactly what he had in mind for that class. He responds that he was referring to a class that represents the system itself, the one that interacts with the user and is responsible for library functions such as checking items in and out. But Betty, who suggested the Librarian class, claims that his description fits her class as well. After all, isn't it the Librarian who will actually be responsible for these tasks? The group decides that Librarian will be the class that has the overall responsibility for checking out and checking in library materials. The term Library will be reserved for a description of the entire application.

Jim next wants to know what class actually refers to the things the library contains and lends. Article, item, material, and lendable are all nouns in the requirements but seem to refer to the same thing. The group agrees and then faces the task of choosing one of these, or a new term, to represent the items that can be borrowed from a library. They decide that Article could be confused with a newspaper or magazine article, and that Material and Item are too general. They settle on Lendable as the term best able to describe an item lent at a library. Betty, as the author of the requirements, decides to change the ambiguous wording in the document as well.

Betty next voices confusion about the distinction between User and Borrower. Do they refer to the same abstraction? Jim says he thinks so, but Cecilia, who suggested the Borrower class, disagrees. When she suggested Borrower, she was referring to objects in the application that represent information about library patrons. For example, a Borrower object would know how many books it has out and which ones. The User, on the other hand, she views as the person using the library, which is probably outside the scope of the system. The group is convinced by her arguments.

The final question comes from Nancy about Due Date and Fine. She questions whether these represent classes of objects that play roles in the system or whether they are actually objects that will be attributes of other classes. She also reminds the group that Wirfs-Brock[4] explicitly says to model types of attributes, not the attributes themselves. Dewey agrees, saying that Due Date is probably an attribute of Lendable and that Fine is really just an attribute of Borrower. Perhaps there is a Date class of which due date is an object. The group decides that it will add a Date class to the model, but that no new class is necessary to represent the values of a fine.

During the filtering stage, the group eliminates the Library, Article, Material, Item, Due Date, and Fine classes and adds a Date class. Thus, they have settled on the following set of classes: Librarian, Lendable, Book, Video, Journal, Date, Borrower, and User.

ASSIGNING CARDS

The classes, each of which becomes a CRC card, can be assigned as they are suggested (usually to the person who suggests them) or later after most classes have been discovered. The latter will probably result in a more equitable distribution of cards. Waiting until later to do the assignment also assures that the filtering of classes has been done before cards are written up. It also keeps the focus of the team on the group activity while the brainstorming takes place. Once team members start worrying about what to write on their cards, they may drop out of the brainstorming process.

The assignment of cards to participants is sometimes based on who knows the most about an abstraction or who will be responsible for a particular abstraction throughout the design and development of the system. For the Library application modeling, Betty takes the Librarian card since she will be the most familiar with the operations it performs. Dewey gets Lendable, seen as a key card for the functioning of the Library. Cecilia seems to have a intuitive feeling about the Borrower class, and she did suggest it. So she is assigned the Borrower and User cards. It seems to make sense to give Book, Video, and Journal to the same person, since they probably have much in common, so Jim gets all of these cards. That just leaves the Date card, which Jim says he will also take.

Each participant takes index cards, which they annotate with the class names they have been assigned. They also write a short precise description of the class on the back of each card. They read these descriptions to the group for approval and mutual understanding. Figure 3.2 shows the back of each card with the descriptions in place.

Superclasses and Subclasses

There is some disagreement as to whether superclasses and subclasses should be identified up front, derived later, or ignored altogether in a CRC card session. In the analysis stage of the sessions, I encourage groups to identify this relationship if it feels obvious to them. For example, when modeling a chess game, it may seem obvious that a Rook is a kind of Chess Piece. If this information is part of a group's understanding of the problem, then it should be noted as such. Disregarding this or any information is counterproductive.

If, however, the group is not certain whether or not this relationship exists, it is better to keep classes separate and see if a superclass relationship arises out of the scenarios. If the classes are assigned behavior that is the same to a large extent, this behavior can be grouped into a superclass. Assuming this relationship too early may force a particular design and bias the distribution of responsibilities. Also, using separate cards for the walkthroughs of the scenarios emphasizes the fact that in many hierarchies it is the objects of the subclasses, not the superclass, that will actually be doing the work of the system. The superclass often just provides a way to refer to any of the subclass objects. This understanding can be lost when the superclass relationship is assumed too early.

Responsibilities

Once a reasonable set of classes are suggested, filtered, and well understood by everyone in the room, it is time to start assigning them the behaviors that will combine to provide

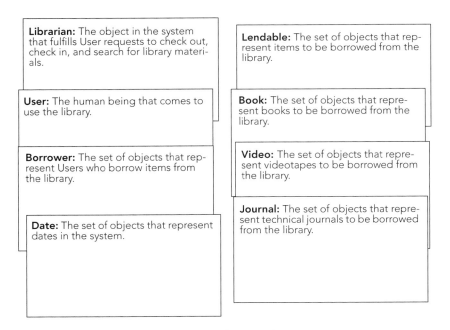

Figure 3.2 Class descriptions written on the backs of CRC cards.

the functions of the application. Single responsibilities, which are derived from the requirements, or responsibilities that are "obvious" from the name of the class can be listed even before scenario execution is begun. For example, the Library group has already decided that Librarian will be responsible for checking lendables in and out. The advantage of assigning these responsibilities early on is that when you execute scenarios, some responsibilities are already in place. However, it is more likely that the cards will contain responsibilities that are not necessary to solve the problem at hand if an attempt is made to assign responsibilities before walking through scenarios.

For example, consider the Librarian class in the Library system. In isolation, we might want to assign the responsibility *Say "shhhh"* to the Librarian class (everyone knows from his or her own experience that librarians all say "shhhh") or *create overdue notices*. But these responsibilities of the Librarian might be extraneous to the functioning of the system under consideration. If we discover in later sessions that they will be useful for the application, we can add them as we need to. But it is best to start with a minimum set of responsibilities. It is an easy matter to add behavior. Walking through a model to delete unused responsibilities is much harder.

Assigning a responsibility from a requirements document ensures that it will be a pertinent behavior in the system under consideration. However, sifting through requirements assigning independent responsibilities without seeing how it fits into the larger picture gets boring. Participants can get itchy waiting to see how they will be used. Exercising very small scenarios (where some collaboration is needed) is a better way to start. The impact or role of the cards, except as a recording mechanism, only becomes clear once scenario execution has begun.

Attributes

Attributes may also be identified by reading the requirements. Often nouns that are not classes but characteristics of classes are best represented as attributes. Due Date and Fine are pertinent examples from the Library domain. Attributes can be assigned to classes as discovered, but this should be done in moderation.

It is important to understand that the emphasis and the strength of the CRC card technique in particular and responsibility-driven design in general lies in deriving the behavior of the class, not the structure. Information necessary to the functioning of the system will be reflected in responsibilities that maintain that information. Names such as *know due date* signal these types of responsibilities. We will use *know* to reflect the responsibility to provide or change the knowledge. For example, we will see during scenario execution that it will be necessary for the Book class to *know due date* in order to determine if a book is overdue or calculate the Fine for an overdue book. *Know* responsibilities may correspond to actual attributes or simply to the ability to get the information when asked for it.

The eventual assignment of attributes is done to support the responsibilities and represents decisions about how the responsibilities are achieved. Because of this, attribute assignment becomes more relevant during the design and implementation phases. As attributes spring to mind in problem modeling, they can be noted; however, time-consuming attempts to independently define a class in terms of its attributes are counter to the process described here.

As with non–scenario-driven assignment of responsibilities, assigning attributes in isolation can result in extraneous information. Waiting to assign attributes ensures that they exist only to support behavior derived earlier. For example, when we think about a Book object in isolation, many different attributes may spring to mind. Title, author, Dewey Decimal number, number of pages, and in or out status, for instance, all may be characteristics that define a book. But which will be important in supporting the activities of checking out and returning books or searching for books? Which will be needed to support operations defined later, such as adding new books to the collection or sending out bills to organizations? The best way to determine which attributes are appropriate for a Book is by first executing scenarios and seeing what behavior is necessary to get the job done.

Scenarios

We now embark on the heart of the CRC card session—the walk-throughs of the application driven by scenarios. We start to assign responsibilities to the classes by simulating what the system is to do by physically moving and embellishing the cards.

Scenarios are detailed examples of the functions of the system. A function does not refer here to a procedural block; rather, it is a single, visible, testable behavior [5]. A function is analogous to a system requirement. Functions describe what happens in the system from a high-level, user point of view. For each function, a set of scenarios exists that explores what would happen given different parameters. For example, the functions of the Library application are checking out an item, returning an item, and searching for an item. But we will walk through many scenarios for each function before we are convinced that we have modeled the system completely.

Scenarios do not have to be any particular length. For example, in the Library application, one can imagine an "end-to-end" scenario covering the time from when the user arrives to check out a book to when that user leaves with the book. But even the "subactivity" of calculating a due date for the book can be considered a scenario. The Library example is so small that our scenarios will seem to be end to end, but any system activity that requires at least one collaboration between objects will be considered a scenario in a CRC card session. In complicated systems, it is a good idea to do shorter "inside" scenarios first, in order to decrease the work when longer encompassing scenarios are executed. We will take advantage of this nesting relationship among scenarios when we document a CRC card design in Chapter 5.

WHERE TO START

Scenarios to be explored are the "what happens when"s that illustrate the expected use of the system. For example, "What happens when Stephanie Ross returns a video, *Introduction to C++*, to the Librarian?" is a potential scenario for the Library application. A group should model the least complicated scenarios first. Chances are that the more difficult and complex situations have components that are simpler scenarios. When the simpler scenarios have been modeled, the responsibilities that support these will be in place to support the more complex situations, allowing the groups to concentrate only on the parts that are more complicated.

Scenarios should be very specific, and related scenarios should be modeled separately. If a group tries to model the system function of returning an item to the library with just one scenario, then within the execution of the scenario they must consider many different branches of possibilities. Questions such as, "What if the item is a Book?" "What if the item is a Video?" and "What if there is more than one item?" arise. This makes each walkthrough much more work and increases the possibility of getting "lost" along the way.

Instead, many different situations should be modeled, e.g., "What happens when Chris Ziegler returns the book *How to Find Carmen Sandiago*?" "What happens when Katie Hayes returns the video *OOP Made Easy*?" etc. You may recognize generalities in responsibilities even in specific instances. If not, they will become clear as more scenarios are executed. Modeling so many similar scenarios separately may seem tedious, but that is deceptive. You will discover that when a related scenario is executed, many of the necessary responsibilities already exist to fulfill it. Only responsibilities representing the essential differences in the situations are revealed.

GUIDELINES FOR SCENARIO EXECUTION

The simulation of the scenarios should be dynamic and anthropomorphic. The people who own particular cards should hold the card in the air and "become" the object when a scenario causes control to pass to them. The set of cards on the table provides a static picture of the classes of objects within the system and the relationships among the classes. While executing scenarios, cards are raised to simulate the dynamic behavior of the system where messages are sent to actual objects performing their tasks. Thus, a card is a class when on the table and an object when in the air.

As each separate action supporting the scenario is identified, it is assigned to a particular card as a responsibility. Raising and lowering cards during a walk-through of a scenario provides important visual cues about the execution of the model. Holding the cards in the air also allows participants to identify more strongly with the abstraction and to become actively immersed in the objectness of the problem. Kent Beck reports some amazing transformations when people actually hold, rather than just point to, their cards[6].

There are no hard and fast rules for the walk-throughs. Nothing dictates exactly what scenarios are performed or exactly what text is written on the card. Groups should do what makes the session flow for them. More rigorous organization of the cards can occur after the session.

CHECK-OUT SCENARIO

In the modeling of the Library application, we have the following set of cards: User, Librarian, Lendable, Book, Video, Journal, Date, and Borrower. The group has not added any independent responsibilities or attributes to the cards. The first scenario chosen for the Library application is simple and specific. "What happens when Barbara Stewart, who has no accrued fines and one outstanding book, not overdue, checks out a book entitled *Effective C++ Strategies*?" Nancy, who has volunteered as session scribe, writes this scenario down just as they have verbalized it. She reminds the group that to simulate the execution of the scenario, it is necessary to identify each task needed to accomplish it and then assign that task to the class best equipped to handle it.

First of all, who should have the overall responsibility for checking out Barbara's book? Betty suggests that the group has already indicated that Librarian will be responsible for this. The group agrees, so Betty writes *check out book* in the responsibility column on her card. Betty, looking at her collaborator column, wonders whose help she needs to accomplish this. Nancy suggests that the answer to this question will depend on what other tasks are involved in checking out a book.

What does checking out a book entail? Betty suggests that there must be a Book object in the system which represents the physical book, *Effective C++ Strategies.* She claims that checking the book out involves changing this Book object in a specific way. Dewey agrees, but reminds her that she must first make sure that the person checking out the book doesn't have overdue books, too large a fine, or too many items out already.

How should this check be done, and whose help does the Librarian need to do it? Dewey suggests that the User could supply this information. Cecilia quickly interrupts. The User is the person coming to the Library and so is outside the software system. There will be a Borrower object that represents information the system has about the User. The Borrower object in this scenario has knowledge about Barbara Stewart. Cecilia claims that she (as Borrower) can help Librarian to verify the user's status. Betty agrees. She lifts her card and the scenario begins as follows:

> **Librarian:** I need to verify that this user does not have any overdue items, does not owe more than $100 dollars in fines, and is not over the lending limit. I will collaborate with Borrower to do this. Borrower, lift your card up.
>
> **Borrower:** I am listing *can borrow* on my card as the corresponding responsibility. I will raise my card as I provide this service. I can use a *know fine* responsibility to see that my fine is less than $100. Now I need to check if I am over my lendable limit or if any of my previously borrowed items is overdue. I can carry this out if I know what I already have checked out. So I will also add a *know set of books* responsibility. Knowing this, I can figure out that I have only one book out. But then I need to find out if the book is overdue. Will you know that, Book?
>
> **Book:** Yes, I was just picking up my card. I should know my due date. I'll add *know due date* as a responsibility. I will also add *know if overdue*. To figure out if I am overdue, I'll keep my card up and collaborate with Date to compare today's date and my due date.
>
> **Date:** I can do that. I will add a *compare dates* responsibility to my list, then raise my card to do it. I guess I need to collaborate with another instance of myself to do this, so I will add Date as my collaborator. In this case, today's date is less than your due date, Book. So I report that to you and put my card down.
>
> **Book:** Great. Borrower, I can tell you that I am not overdue. And then I'm finished for the time being.
>
> **Borrower:** Right. Librarian, the Borrower can borrow. Now I can put my card back on the table.

Dewey stops the scenario at this point to ask a question. So far, Librarian collaborates with Borrower, who in turn collaborates with Book, who collaborates with Date. Shouldn't there be collaborations in the opposite direction? That is, shouldn't Borrower add a collaboration with Librarian as it tells her that it is OK for the Borrower to borrow?

Nancy remarks that this is an excellent question and an important point. The answer is no, collaborations as noted on CRC cards are one-way relationships from the client to the server. When Librarian asks Borrower whether it can borrow, this collaboration assumes that it will receive an answer as a result of the request. No separate message or collaboration is necessary to send the answer back.

Back to the check-out scenario—Nancy asks what needs to happen next. Again, Betty indicates that the next steps are to change the Book's state to indicate that it is OUT. She suggests that she will need to collaborate with Book three times to set its due date, in or out status, and borrower. Nancy interrupts with a question. Why does Betty think that these pieces of knowledge (due date, borrower, and in or out status) will be important for Book to have? Betty responds that in her experience, this set of information is pertinent. They've already seen that Book needs to *know its due date.* In or out status will be important to people looking for a book. And a future activity such as creating overdue notices will require knowledge of the Borrower, she is sure. Since the information is here, why not save it? The group bows to her experience and domain expertise.

Jim remarks that he agrees that this information is important, but that it seems as if Betty sees Book as a passive repository of this information that Librarian simply queries to do the task. He argues that, since he (as Book) has all the necessary knowledge at his disposal, he should just do the checking out. Betty argues that a higher intelligence may be needed to order the subtasks.

In the face of the stalemate, a silence falls over the room, and Nancy jumps in. The first rule, she claims, is that when deadlock is reached, any decision is usually better than none, even if the choice does not turn out to be the optimal one or the permanent one. Go down one path for a while and examine the downstream implications as they occur. If the decision turns out to be a mistake, it is easy enough to fix. Exploring and making mistakes is an integral part of the CRC card process. Models can be changed at the drop of a card.

In this case, however, she has some useful advice. The question at hand is how the actual checking out of the book takes place. The choices are as follows:

- The Librarian could ask Book to do the various subtasks involved as part of its responsibility to *check out a book.*

- Book could have the responsibility to check itself out, and the subtasks could be private responsibilities that it has in order to fulfill this *check out* responsibility.

Why not execute the scenario both ways and see which makes more sense? The important thing to look for is whether Librarian has some knowledge or ability in terms of ordering or interpreting the tasks that requires that she have access to Book's information. If so, then the Librarian must own the responsibility and should gather what she needs to do her job. Otherwise, Book should probably check itself out to limit Librarian's reliance on Book's internal knowledge.

As project members execute each mini-scenario, they can visually see the collaborations. In the first possibility:

> **Librarian:** As part of my responsibility to check out this book for this User, I need to ask the Book object to calculate and update its due date. Book?
>
> **Book:** Okay, I know my due date is today's date plus 4 weeks, since I'm a book, so I will add *calculate due date* to my responsibility list, and I have *know due date* already. Then I'll raise my card and do it.
>
> **Librarian:** Good. Now I need to ask you to update your borrower knowledge to this Borrower.
>
> **Book:** Okay, I added *know borrower* to my list, and now I will bring my card up and I will set that field. Back to you, Librarian.
>
> **Librarian:** Now Book, I next need you to change your in or out status to OUT.
>
> **Book:** And again I will add that responsibility (*know in or out*), and again I will rise to the occasion.

Now let us examine the second possibility as a scenario where Book is assigned the *check-out* responsibility:

> **Librarian:** I have the responsibility to check out this book for this User. Book, if I tell you who the Borrower is, can you please check yourself out? Book?
>
> **Book:** Sure, I can rise to that occasion. I must know how to *calculate my due date* (today's date plus 4 weeks) and I need to *know borrower*, *know due date*, and *know in or out*. I will add these as responsibilities. Okay, done. Back to you, Librarian.

Clearly, the first approach causes a higher degree of coupling between Librarian and Book than the second scenario. And Betty admits that there does not seem to be any special knowledge that the Librarian brings to the task. This, plus the fact that the first alternative implies that Librarian needs to know too much about Book's internal state, sways the group in favor of the second alternative. Jim points out that, using this approach, changing Book's representation in the future will not affect the way Librarian carries out her responsibilities. This is one of the advantages for maintainability that they are trying to gain with an object-oriented approach.

Cecilia then reminds the group that the scenario is not finished. She (as Borrower) needs to know that she has an additional Book checked out. Dewey asks why she thinks she needs this knowledge. Cecilia reminds him that she has the responsibility to *know set of books* so that she can determine if she has any overdue items or is at her ending limit. These were responsibilities she wrote down in support of the *can borrow* responsibility as the first step of this scenario. Her question at this stage is, who should be responsible for telling Borrower to update its knowledge about outstanding Lendables?

This question turns out to be a controversial one. Cecilia and Jim think that Book should notify the Borrower that it has the book as an outstanding lendable. They argue that it knows the Borrower and so might as well take care of this as part of checking itself out. Dewey and Betty represent the other side of the issue. They think that Librarian should have this responsibility. They argue that Librarian already collaborates with Borrower to check if it can borrow.

Cecilia and Jim counter with the fact that Book could also check borrower's status as part of the check-out responsibility. Betty agrees that it could, but if so, Book becomes involved even if it turns out that Borrower cannot check it out! In her model, a Book object only comes into play if it is actually going to be checked out. Dewey finishes by saying that it simply feels more natural to him to have Book be responsible only for maintaining its information and for Librarian to interact with the Borrower.

The group turns to Nancy for advice. Which is right? She reiterates that there are many different ways to model a problem, many only slightly better than others. Some decisions may feel more natural. Others may have trade-offs in terms of reusability or eventual performance implications. In this case, she admits that she is leaning toward Dewey and Betty's model because it implies fewer collaboration paths. The group decides to follow that model, but notes the alternative design for future consideration.

So Librarian will finish her *check out book* responsibility by telling Borrower to add the Book to her list. Betty and Cecilia conclude as follows:

Librarian: I will now inform the Borrower about this Book as the last step in my *check book out for user* responsibility. And I will collaborate with Borrower to do that.

Borrower: And I will add a responsibility to *add Book to set of Books*. No, I think my *know set of Books* responsibility should handle this update also. I will just raise my card and do it.

As they finish, Jim asks Cecilia why she doesn't list Book as a collaborator for her responsibility *know set of books.* Cecilia reminds him that collaborations are not usually needed for responsibilities that simply hold information. She says that Borrower does not need Book's help to just put a Book in a set. Nancy agrees, verifying that collaborations will be used only for situations where an object actually sends a message to a collaborator.

   Thus, the group finishes simulating the execution of their first scenario. Generally the first scenario takes the longest to walk-through. This is because every responsibility is new and must be added. Ground rules are set, and the framework for the overall behavior of the system is put into place. Also, people are just beginning to understand and get comfortable with the process and the interactions. Additional scenario simulations benefit from the work done in the first walk-through and generally take much less time to complete. Figure 3.3 shows the set of cards annotated so far.

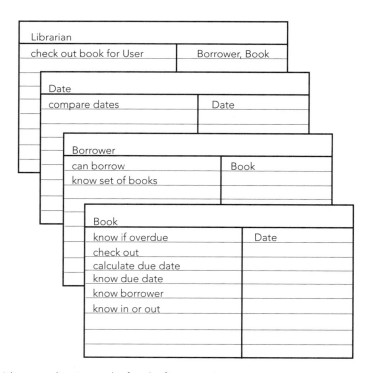

Figure 3.3 Library application cards after the first scenario.

SUPERCLASS DISCOVERY

Next, the group decides to do a similar and related scenario, "What happens when Bronwyn Glor, who has one outstanding book, not overdue, checks out the video *A Basic, Visual Introduction to Visual Basic*?"

> **Librarian:** Okay, I have my card up, as usual. I have added the responsibility *check out video for user*. First I will verify that the User doesn't have any overdue Lendables and is not at her lending limit. To do this, I collaborate with Borrower.
>
> **Borrower:** Yes, and I have the necessary responsibilities (*can borrow*) in place to answer that question for you. And it looks like I'm OK. Back to you, Librarian.
>
> **Librarian:** Now Video, if I tell you who the Borrower is, can you please check yourself out?
>
> **Video:** Sure, I can do that. I'll add *check out* to my card. I know how to *calculate due date* (today's date plus 7 days) and I *know due date*, *know borrower*, and *know in or out*. I will add these as responsibilities. Okay, done. Back to you, Librarian. Oh wait, I forgot. I have to collaborate with myself (as Date, that is) to calculate my due date. So I'll add that collaboration.
>
> **Date:** And I'll hold up my card after I add my responsibility *add days to date*.
>
> **Book:** And I'll add that collaboration to my incarnation as Book as well because we forgot that during the last scenario.
>
> **Librarian:** Now Borrower, I need to inform you about this new Video. This all seems familiar. Hmm. Somehow I have the feeling that this scenario will be the same no matter what the User is checking out. Perhaps I should replace *check out book* and *check out video* with a more general responsibility *check out lendable*.
>
> **Borrower:** Good idea. Then I can replace my *know set of books* with the more general responsibility *know set of lendables*.

The group has noticed the similarity in the first two scenarios. This is clear from Betty and Cecilia's desire to change the wording of their responsibilities. The structure of the scenarios is almost identical, and many of the necessary responsibilities already exist. The only difference between them is the type of Lendable involved and how the due date gets calculated. Rather than do the same scenario with a Journal, they simply write the corresponding responsibilities on the Journal card.

Dewey is becoming suspicious about the utility of his Lendable card. He has noticed that no matter what gets checked out of the Library, a Lendable card does not actually come into play. He wonders if they should discard it. Jim interrupts, saying that he has a better idea. All of his cards—Book, Video, and Journal—have the same set of responsibilities. Perhaps they can factor up these responsibilities and put them into a superclass. Lendable seems to fit the bill for this superclass since each of the other classes "is a kind of" Lendable. Some responsibilities, such as *check out, know borrower, know if overdue, know due date*, and *know in or out* will be carried out the same way no matter what type of Lendable is doing it; these will be listed only on the Lendable card. Others, such as *calculate due date*, are carried out differently by different subclasses. These types of responsibilities can be written on the cards for each subclass as well as for Lendable so that it is clear that they do these things in their own special way.

The group is enthusiastic, especially Dewey, who has not had a chance to raise a card. Nancy apologizes to Dewey but says that the entire set of cards for the hierarchy should be owned by the same person. She thinks that it makes sense for that person to be Jim, since he has been working with the cards. Jim offers Dewey the Date card in exchange. Jim then takes all the cards for the Lendable class hierarchy and rewrites each, putting the

Figure 3.4 Lendable hierarchy.

responsibilities where they should be and noting superclass and subclass relationships on the cards. Other participants check their responsibilities and reword them, where appropriate, to say lendable rather than book, video, or journal. Betty notes that this will make it easier to adapt the model to handle new types of Lendables that have their own characteristics and behavior. Dewey mentions that this will be important when they add Books-On-Tape to the Library next spring. Figure 3.4 shows the cards for the new Lendable hierarchy.

RELATED SCENARIOS

The group does a few more related scenarios until they are sure that they have recorded most of the responsibilities needed for the normal functioning of checking out lendables. For example, Cecilia wonders how her *can borrow* responsibility would differ if Barbara had more than one Lendable at home. Nancy suggests they do the short scenario associated with Borrower's verification of the User status that is part of the following "What happens when Dave Annatone, with no fine and a nonoverdue journal and video at home, decides to check out the book *CRC to C++*?"

> **Borrower:** I already have *can borrow* on my card and *know set of lendables* responsibility. I can figure out that I have two Lendables out, which is within my lending limit. Then I need to know if either is overdue. Can I ask each one? Journal?
>
> **Journal:** Yes, I know my due date. I have a responsibility, *know if overdue*, that I inherited from Lendable. To fulfill this, I will keep my card up and collaborate with Date to compare today's date and my due date.
>
> **Date:** I will use my *compare dates* responsibility and do the comparison. Book, in this case, today's date is less than the overdue date.
>
> **Journal:** Great. Borrower, I am not overdue.
>
> **Borrower:** How about you, Video.
>
> **Video:** I have this responsibility, since it is on the Lendable card. I will collaborate with Date and let you know.
>
> **Date:** No, I have compared the dates, and you are not overdue either.
>
> **Video:** Great. Borrower, I am not overdue.
>
> **Borrower:** Right. Librarian, the Borrower status is okay.

Situations such as checking out multiple books or multiple lendables of different types also go smoothly with the responsibilities that already exist.

RETURN SCENARIOS

Comfortable that they have covered the necessary check-out situations, the group tries a simple scenario for returning a lendable. "What happens when Liz Flanagan returns her book, *Barely Managing O-O Projects*, on time?" What needs to happen in order to help a user check in a book? Betty offers to take this responsibility and begins the execution of the scenario.

> **Librarian:** First, I add *check in lendable* to my card. Then I need to collaborate with you, Book. I need to know if you are overdue. Are you overdue?
>
> **Book:** Okay, I already have the responsibility, *know if overdue*, inherited from Lendable. I again need to collaborate with Date to compare my due date with today's date. Date?
>
> **Date:** I can do that. In this case, today's date is less than the due date.
>
> **Book:** Okay, that means that in this case, Librarian, I am not overdue.
>
> **Librarian:** Good. Book, raise your card and check yourself in!
>
> **Book:** I sure will. I will add the *check in* responsibility to my base class, since all Lendables will do this the same way. I need to update my in or out status to IN and update my borrower and due date knowledge to empty. And I already have the *know* responsibilities to do all this. Back to you, Librarian.
>
> **Librarian:** Borrower, I need to collaborate with you to inform you that you no longer have this book out.
>
> **Borrower:** I will find *know set of lendables* on my list of responsibilities. Then I will raise my card and do it!

Note that the check-in scenario simulation generated a few extra responsibilities. But most of the necessary behavior was already in place.

EXCEPTIONAL SCENARIOS

A group should always execute easy and nonexceptional scenarios first. Why make life difficult early on by contemplating situations that will occur infrequently? Only when a working model of the system exists and handles the normal activity should exceptional scenarios be explored.

For example, "What happens when Gregg Vesonder tries to check out a journal, *Genetic Programming in Your Spare Time*, when he already has 5 volumes of the same journal at home?" How does that fit into the current model? In the past set of scenarios, the Borrower's check of the User's status has always gone smoothly. How does the model hold up when this case is considered? The group walks through this scenario as follows:

> **Borrower:** In this case, since I have a *know set of lendables* responsibility, I know that I am at my lendable limit. And I will report this to you, Librarian.
>
> **Librarian:** Since Borrower is at its lendable limit, I will need to alert the User that they cannot check anything out and end the session.

Cecilia suggests that Betty add *display message* to her responsibilities in order to handle this. Maybe she could just write User Interface or UI Subsystem as her collaborator, as a placeholder. Nancy affirms that it is a good idea to write the name of a collaborating subsystem at the point of collaboration. This makes it clear that Librarian will serve as an interface between the subsystems in the problem model.

The group is encouraged that the exceptional check-out scenario added one more responsibility to the cards, but otherwise fit in seamlessly.

Cecilia next wants to try an exceptional return scenario, "What happens when Garrett Ziegler returns a video, *Introduction to Interactive Television*, 3 days overdue?"

> **Book:** My *know if overdue* responsibility will discover that I am now overdue, Librarian.
>
> **Librarian:** In that case, I guess I need to charge the user a fine. Book, I will ask you to calculate this fine for me.
>
> **Book:** I can do that. I will add *calculate fine* to the card for every kind of Lendable, since we will all do it a different way. OK, the fine amount in this case is $15, Librarian!
>
> **Librarian:** I will also ask Borrower to record the fact that Garrett owes $15 so that his organization can be billed at the end of the month.
>
> **Borrower:** I already have a *know fine amount* responsibility. Back to you, Librarian.
>
> **Librarian:** I also want Garrett to know that I have charged him a fine. Maybe I can use my *display message* responsibility to do this. Then I will continue the check-in process as before.

Cecilia wonders if they should next do a scenario for billing of organizations that was touched upon in this scenario. Dewey argues that billing will be done by a different application. Finding overdue books might also fall into that auditing application. They decided at the beginning of the session to model checking in, checking out, and searching for books, and he suggests they stick with that plan. The group agrees. An updated version of the cards appears in Figure 3.5.

Adding exceptional scenarios in this application has been relatively painless because the responsibilities are in place to handle most of what needs to be done. Sometimes, however, dealing with exceptional cases can cause more dramatic changes to a model.

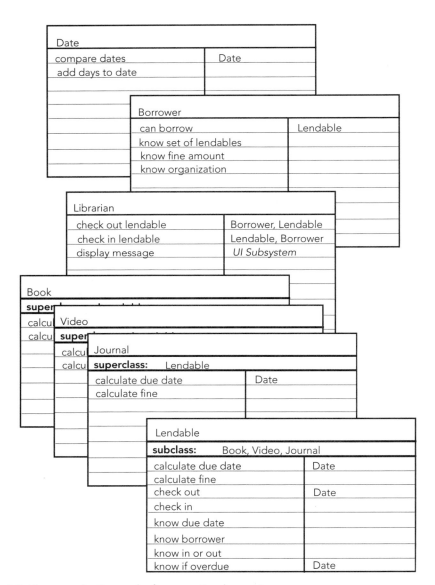

Date	
compare dates	Date
add days to date	

Borrower	
can borrow	Lendable
know set of lendables	
know fine amount	
know organization	

Librarian	
check out lendable	Borrower, Lendable
check in lendable	Lendable, Borrower
display message	*UI Subsystem*

Book	
super	
calcu	
calcu	

Video	
super	
calcu	
calcu	

Journal	
superclass: Lendable	
calculate due date	Date
calculate fine	

Lendable	
subclass: Book, Video, Journal	
calculate due date	Date
calculate fine	
check out	Date
check in	
know due date	
know borrower	
know in or out	
know if overdue	Date

Figure 3.5 Library application cards after exceptional scenarios.

Discovering New Classes

Often, as scenarios are executed, a group realizes that none of the classes on the table is appropriate to house a particular responsibility. This spurs the creation of a new class with the appropriate behavior.

When the Library group has executed a fairly complete set of normal and exceptional scenarios for checking out and returning library lendables, they branch out into searching scenarios. Nancy suggests that they walk through the following situation: "What happens when Ned Brooks comes to the Library in search of a book entitled *The Mythical Mammoth*?" Betty lifts her card and begins:

> **Librarian:** I will take the responsibility, *search for lendable*. But where do I look? Whose help do I need? How about you, Book?
>
> **Book:** I can't look for myself. In past scenarios, you knew which book object was involved. But now, you need someone to look over a set of Books to find the correct one. I can't do that.

Dewey points out that there is no existing class that can handle this task. He is amazed that they have totally excluded any abstraction that deals with the collection of lendables in the Library. He volunteers enthusiastically to become a Collection class. He grabs a card while the group wonders how they could have missed this class. Nancy assures them that it is not likely that they could identify all classes at the beginning. It is necessary to go through many scenarios to be sure you have all the classes. This is part of what a CRC card session is all about. Then they begin again:

> **Librarian:** It is my responsibility to find this book. Collection, can you help me?
>
> **Collection:** Yes, I will add *know set of lendables* to my responsibility list. This may mean that I have this set as part of my knowledge or that I know which database table to search, but we will deal with this design issue later. Eventually, I have to deal with the database, though, so I think that I will add DB Subsystem as a collaborator for this responsibility. And I need to collaborate with each Book object to get information to see if it is the one I am looking for.
>
> **Book:** That also implies that I have a *know title* responsibility. In fact, I must have the responsibility to know about anything a User might use to search for a Book.
>
> **Collection:** Actually, you need to know about anything the User would search on OR want to see displayed about you. Anyway, once I find the Book, I can return it to you, Librarian.
>
> **Librarian:** And I will need to get this information to the User. I will use *display message* from my list of responsibilities. Again, I guess I can write UI Subsystem as my collaborator.

The group decides to determine what information each Lendable will need to have in order to support searching. They decide that, rather than write a *know* responsibility for each attribute in Lendable's information set, they will represent the information as attributes on the back of the cards. They feel that attributes here will add to the analysis and their understanding of the problem domain.

They start with Book. What attributes of a book, aside from the ones that make it lendable, will be important for users to see and use for searching? Certainly title and author come to mind. For display, the user might want to see publisher and publication date, says Betty. Is publisher really important for a Library, asks Nancy? Dewey says that it is important because people do a search at the library to get information with which to order books. Cecilia adds that some indication of location will be important so that the user can locate the book. But Dewey claims that the Dewey Decimal number should work for that.

Jim thinks that some of these attributes should actually be attributes of Lendable. Won't all Lendables have a Dewey Decimal number, just as they all have an in or out status? These are really just attributes that make them lendable rather than part of the intrinsic nature of the item itself. The other attributes, even where there are apparent similarities (such as title or name), Jim votes to leave as part of the Book class, simply to emphasize this distinction. The group agrees, then goes through the same exercise with Journal and Video. Figure 3.6 shows the back of the Lendable, Book, Journal, and Video cards once the Library team is finished assigning attributes.

Jim interrupts the group with a point. Since Librarian needs to tell Collection to retrieve a Lendable based on certain criteria, doesn't it need to get information from the User? Betty agrees and says she will add *get info from user* to her card. Again she will add the UI Subsystem as her collaborator. Cecilia notes that although they didn't model this directly in the check-in and check-out scenarios, Librarian already needs this capability to determine who the User is and what they are checking out. This will be modeled more completely in design.

Cecilia mentions another interesting fact that occurred to her as she watched Librarian get a Lendable object from Collection in the previous scenario. Librarian probably had to talk to some Collection to get the Lendable object for check-out and check-in as well. Wouldn't the Librarian get the Lendable ID from the User and ask Collection for the actual object? Jim thinks that the Lendable object would actually talk to a Collection object or the database as part of its create responsibility. Either way, this is a design decision that should be argued in the sessions to follow. So the group makes a note of it and agrees to table that discussion for a short while.

Armed with their updated set of classes and responsibilities, the group asks Nancy to read her list of scenarios, and they run through each of the ones executed so far. Everything runs smoothly and the model holds up nicely. They begin to feel as if they are converging on a stable model.

Grouping Cards

The placement of CRC cards on the table provides a visual representation of the emerging model. The groupings physically mimic the relationships between classes. Hierarchies of classes, for example, Lendable and its subclasses, are often stacked on the table. They should at least be placed very close together. This is why they should always be owned by the same person.

Other classes that collaborate heavily should also be close together on the table to accentuate the amount of cooperation between them. Some classes include objects of other classes in their state. This relationship is referred to as a "has-a" relationship and is sometimes evident by looking at where their associated cards lie. This is especially true

Lendable: The set of objects that represent items to be borrowed from the library.

Attributes:

| in or out status | due date |
| borrower | dewey decimal # |

Book: The set of objects that represent books to be borrowed from the library.

Attributes:

| title | pub. date |
| author | **publisher** |

Journal: The set of objects that represent journals to be borrowed from the library.

Attributes:

| name | volume |
| date | **issue** |

Video: The set of objects that represent videos to be borrowed from the library.

Attributes:

| title | date |
| vhs or beta | producer |

Figure 3.6 CRC cards with some attributes noted on the back.

if no other classes collaborate with the owned class. For instance, in the Library application, the Date card is placed very close to the Lendable hierarchy because an object of type Date is an attribute of Lendable. Participants may have to exchange cards and change places at the table to reflect these relationships.

Card clustering based on heavy usage or collaborations can provide visual clues to subsystems. For sessions where subsystems are not evident beforehand, they can begin to emerge in the cards based on physical proximity. In these situations the subdividing of the problem is a result of, rather than an input to, the CRC card session.

Enhancements to the Basic Process

The process we have described—brainstorming and filtering classes, noting attributes where helpful, and "executing" scenarios to discover responsibilities and collaborations— form the core of the CRC card session. Rigorous scenario execution using the framework of brainstormed classes will eventually cause the convergence to a working model of the system. Other activities, however, can be added to the process and the session to help form the model in a healthy way.

SCENARIO LIST

An important addition to the basic CRC card process is the recording of the scenarios as they are suggested and executed. A group will undoubtedly want to use this list throughout the sessions. Scenarios may need to be reexecuted to check a new model or design when significant changes take place in the cards. The list can also be used to illustrate to others the way in which the model can be exercised to fulfill the workings of the system. Therefore, it is an important part of the documentation of a CRC card design (see Chapter 5). This list will eventually be used as the basis for a set of test cases for the working system (see Chapter 6).

COLLABORATION DRAWINGS

Grouping cards on the table gives the session participants a physical sense of class interactions. But specific collaborations can only be determined by looking at the collaborator column of each card. A helpful exercise as a CRC card session progresses is the placement of the cards on a white board, or somewhere comparable, where collaboration lines can be drawn between them.

This collaboration drawing allows you to see more clearly the sets of interactions. Do subsystems or patterns of collaborations emerge, or does it look like spaghetti? The advantage of doing this in a CRC card session is that some of the lines on the board may surprise some of the people in the room. Drawing collaborations can point out errors in people's perception of a scenario or in the recording process itself. The process of streamlining collaborations by moving responsibilities or creating new classes is also facilitated by this approach.

For example, the Library application group puts its cards on the board, adds the arrows for the collaborations it has recorded, and draws representations for the user interface and data base subsystems. When they finish, they have something that looks like Figure 3.7. Betty and Dewey agree that, from their Library experience, the collaborations look reasonable. Jim adds that he has ideas for design that will change some of the collaborations but is satisfied that this picture captures a good description of what the application will do.

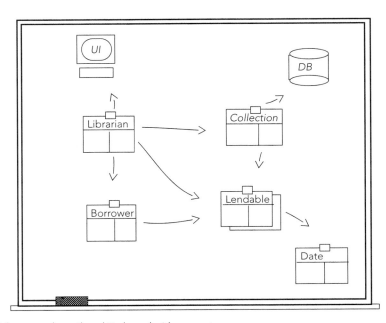

Figure 3.7 Library cards on the white board with magnets.

Nancy suggests that, when looking at a picture such as this, a group should look for cards, or sets of cards, that only have arrows pointing at them and none emanating from them. These classes, or sets of classes, with no outward collaborations are potentially reusable because they require no knowledge of the rest of the application. A simple example in the Library application is the Date class. Lendable collaborates with Date, but Date needs no other class to perform its responsibilities. Therefore, it can be implemented using a generic Date abstraction. Even the Lendable hierarchy may be reusable across Library applications because it requires no knowledge of other Library classes. It relies only on the generic Date abstraction.

Library Cards

The following list of classes, responsibilities, and collaborators represents the entire set (just the front) of CRC cards for the problem-modeling sessions of the Library application.

Librarian

check out lendable	Lendable, Borrower
check in lendable	Lendable, Borrower
search for lendable	Collection
get info from user	UI Subsystem
display message	UI Subsystem

Collection

know set of lendables	DB Subsystem, Lendable

Borrower

can borrow	Lendable
know set of lendables	
know fine amount	

Lendable

subclasses: Book, Video, Journal	
calculate due date	Date
calculate fine	
check out	Date
check in	
know due date	

```
            know borrower
            know in or out
            know if overdue                    Date
```

Book	
superclass: Lendable calculate due date calculate fine	Date

Video	
superclass: Lendable calculate due date calculate fine	Date

Journal	
superclass: Lendable calculate due date calculate fine	Date

Date	
compare dates add days to date	Date

Potential Pitfalls

The CRC card session is informal and fun, and it seems to gain a life of its own as it progresses. However, there are a few situations that can begin to derail a session or stop it dead in its tracks.

Deadlock

Deadlock occurs when two "equally good" ways of modeling the problem present themselves and cause a session to halt. This includes situations in which there are strong proponents arguing for each side as well as situations in which where no one can decide which one is better. Making a suboptimal decision at this point is much better than continuing to cycle or stall. This is especially true because the cost of a "wrong" decision at this stage is fairly low. And the probability of learning the consequences of the error and discovering a better choice later is high.

Flip a coin, take a vote, and continue executing scenarios using that model. It is a good idea, though, to record the choices that you have made. If problems are encountered later whose origins can be traced to a particular choice, you have alternative designs already noted and ready to try.

Where Am I?

The "where-am-I" phenomenon refers to the feeling, deep into the execution of a scenario, that you are at a loss as to what to do next. It usually occurs when you have finished a particularly complicated branch of the execution. There are a few approaches that can help avoid this lost feeling.

First, keeping scenarios as specific as possible helps to minimize the possibility of getting lost because it decreases the number of branches that a group investigates within a single scenario. Next, it is important for anyone whose responsibility is executing to keep their card in the air. This serves as a visual placeholder for the simulation.

Careful ordering of the scenarios can also help reduce the risk of getting lost. If "inner" scenarios (scenarios for sets of operations upon which other scenarios depend) are executed first, longer scenarios will not be as complicated or require adding as many responsibilities. In a long scenario, when a group gets to an operation that has been modeled before, it is not necessary to hold up cards and execute it fully every time. For example, in many of the check out scenarios of the Library application, the execution of *calculate due date* was repeated each time, complete with group members raising their cards. This physical execution could have been skipped to decrease the complexity of encompassing scenarios.

Finally, another approach is to write down "subresponsibilities" even if they are not going to be part of the interface of a class, and always be aware which subresponsibility is being modeled. For example, we noted only *check out lendable* as a Librarian responsibility, not the subtasks of verifying that the Borrower can borrow, asking a lendable to check itself out, and notifying the Borrower about the new lendable. If we had gotten lost after verifying the Borrower status, it would have been helpful to have this step specifically noted, either on the cards or elsewhere. The reader will see that we encourage adding these subresponsibilities to the cards later as a prelude to implementation.

Procedural Thinking

A rather subtle potential pitfall in a CRC card session with a group new to the object-oriented approach is that participants may slide into procedural thinking. A symptom or effect of this is that objects are being viewed as processes. Phrases such as "calling an object" are heard. The idea of many objects of a particular class is lost; that is, classes are being viewed as a single instance that always exists.

A session is especially vulnerable to this phenomenon when the problem being modeled has many classes that will have just one instance in the application. For example, in the Library application, Librarian and Collection, as modeled so far, will most likely have just one instance each. Lendables and Borrowers are more dynamic objects, and different instances of these classes play a part in the scenarios.

To avoid this pitfall and ensure that participants really begin to think in objects, scenarios that emphasize the use of different objects of a class need to be done. This is why the scenarios for the Library application used and identified different specific lendables and borrowers.

Facilitating a CRC Card Session

As previously indicated, a CRC card session benefits from a facilitator knowledgeable in object-oriented technology. The facilitator may be an outside professional or a member of the project team temporarily filling that role. This section contains some tips for the object-oriented expert who wants to facilitate a CRC card session.

If the project team is new to object-oriented technology and CRC cards, the main goal of the facilitator is to teach the group the essence of object-oriented modeling and how to use the CRC card technique to support this modeling. A secondary goal is to help the group develop an object-oriented model for a particular application. The job involves guiding communication, settling controversy, pointing out pros and cons of approaches that are being debated, avoiding repetitive cycles of discussion, getting the group unstuck, and generally keeping the work flowing.

Any facilitator needs some preparation in the domain and should have an idea from reading requirements or other literature what the set of classes is likely to be. But he or she should not enter the session with a straw horse design prepared. Having a prior design may seem to make the session easier because it requires less thinking on the fly during the session. However, it has severe disadvantages. Having a design in mind will bias facilitator feedback during the session and could obscure or discount important issues that argue for alternative models. This biasing of the session is even more counterproductive because such a design is likely to be wanting. It lacks the domain expert input and the breadth of group discussion of alternatives.

Matthew Pittman uses the term "domain idiot" to describe an experienced object-oriented technologist who is intelligent and skilled at development, but who is ignorant of the particular domain under observation. He warns "Beware the domain idiot.... A domain idiot ... naïvely believes that these admirable [object-oriented] qualities equip him to perform a domain analysis in an area in which he has no expertise. Domain idiots tend to oversimplify and to cling to the first good idea they think of"[7]. Domain idiocy may be an advantage when asking questions but is an obvious disadvantage for creating a design solution.

When projects make decisions that the facilitator thinks will lead to trouble, he or she should inform them of the trade-offs and the potential pitfalls that are the implications of their decisions. Group members may change their minds or they might want to continue along the same path. The facilitator should let them do it! First of all, they may be right. But later, if they do run into a problem, this can be identified as a consequence of their earlier decision. Such teaching of the consequences of certain actions in object-oriented modeling, through an example close to home, is very powerful.

Groups sometimes feel lost when the facilitator leaves a set of sessions. This usually suggests that, although an object-oriented model may have been created, the facilitator did not accomplish the goal of transferring his or her knowledge of the CRC card process and object-oriented techniques. If this happens, the project can waiver or fail and abandon the use of the cards and object-oriented technology altogether. If a facilitator participates long enough, even intermittently, for a member of the team to become knowledgeable and comfortable with object-oriented concepts, that member can then assume the role of the expert and facilitate the sessions.

Summing Up

The CRC card session is an animated exchange where applications are modeled by participants "becoming" the objects and role-playing the workings of the system. Some preparation in terms of choosing the participants and narrowing the scope of the problem needs to be done before a session begins. Sessions facilitated by an object-oriented expert are best at helping participants learn the new paradigm and build a good object-oriented model. The order of events in a session is up to each project, but we like to brainstorm classes, then assign cards, then start the execution of scenarios. Listing scenarios and drawing collaboration charts of the emerging objects can aid the process.

Coming Up

In the next chapter we discuss how CRC cards are used to analyze a problem and what to do once a stable problem model is developed.

References

1. Flanagan, Elizabeth, "The Manager's Role." *The C++ Report* 5(7):19–21 (1993).

2. Coplien, James. "Experiences with CRC Cards at AT&T." *The C++ Report* 3(8):1–6 (1991).

3. Stroustrup, Bjarne. *The C++ Programming Language*. Addison-Wesley, Reading, MA, 1991, p. 387.

4. Wirfs-Brock, Rebecca, Lauren Wiener, and Brian Wilkerson. *Designing Object-Oriented Software* p. 39. Prentice Hall, Englewood Cliffs, NJ, 1990.

5. Booch, Grady. *Object-Oriented Analysis and Design with Applications*, 2nd ed. Benjamin/Cummings, Redwood City, CA, 1993.

6. Beck, Kent. "Think Like an Object." *UNIX Review,* 9(10):39–43 (1991).

7. Pittman, Matthew. "Lessons Learned in Managing Object-Oriented Development." *IEEE Software,* pp. 43–47 (January 1993).

CHAPTER
4

CRC Cards for Analysis

a·nal·y·sis *1. the separating of any material or abstract entity into its*

constituent elements. 2. this process as a method of studying the nature of

something or determining its essential features and their relations.

3. a presentation, usually in writing, of the results of this process.

—*Random House Dictionary*
of the English Language[1]

W**HEN BUILDING AN** object-oriented model of an application, the focus of the early CRC card sessions is on analyzing and describing the problem. During this problem-modeling phase, the group identifies entities that are relevant to the application domain. These entities become analysis classes, and the behavior necessary to describe the activity of the system is represented as responsibilities of these classes. Any system activity is the activity of an object, or set of objects, of these classes.

In this chapter, we emphasize the problem-modeling or analysis aspects of CRC cards and the CRC card process. We then discuss various topics of interest during this early phase of the project. We investigate how CRC cards can be used for projects who want to move to object-oriented development but have the constraints of legacy systems. We then discuss reuse considerations in problem modeling. Finally, we explore ways in which CRC cards can contribute to projects using formal methodologies.

Analysis vs. Design

The line where analysis ends and design begins in the lifetime of an application may be somewhat fuzzy. This is true in every project, but especially in small- to medium-sized projects of, say, 2 to 10 team members. In these small-team efforts, the design model may be built directly with no separately produced problem model. Nevertheless, the distinction between which part of the model describes the problem and which describes the solution is an important one.

First of all, the analysis and design represent different views of the system; thus, they form the vocabulary for different groups of people involved in the project. For example, the analysis will have high client visibility. If you need to interact with customers about what the system will do, a separate problem model is important. Classes critical in the design and implementation phases, such as queues and database management interface classes, are meaningless to end users. Also, the makeup of the group in CRC card sessions shifts as it moves from analysis to design. Early sessions that concentrate on problem modeling require more domain expertise than design expertise. As the group moves to solution modeling, the emphasis shifts to design expertise.

Even if no separate problem model is produced, the probability of building the right product will be greater if what the application does is the focus early on and design decisions are made within that framework. For this discussion, we will assume that a stable problem model is reached before the design stage is entered at full steam.

Strengths of CRC Cards for Analysis

CRC cards have particular strengths at each phase of development. The advantages of using the cards for problem modeling are as follows.

Common Project Vocabulary

People from all phases of the project can be involved in CRC card sessions for problem modeling from the outset. Hence, the names of classes and responsibilities are seen, heard, and understood by everyone involved in the project. Most important, these terms are created, debated, and agreed upon by project members at the start of the process. This leads to a common product and project vocabulary across development roles and enhances the concept of a common team goal.

Spreading Domain Knowledge

As we have stated previously, the good news and bad news about objects is that domain entities participate directly in the application, and good or bad domain knowledge has a high impact on the quality of the application. This implies that it is vital for the people building the application to have a good working knowledge of the domain. CRC card sessions get the right people in the room and facilitate discussion. Domain knowledge is spread in a very real way in the sessions because participants actually experience the workings of the system. This serves to teach and clarify in a way that reading requirements or looking at a set of pictures cannot.

Making the Paradigm Shift

The role playing of the system model also facilitates the spread of knowledge about the object-oriented approach to problem modeling. The paradigm shift is internalized by participants through the experimental and experiential nature of the sessions. Every participant is an object, and everything that happens does so because an object makes it happen.

Live Prototyping

At this stage, people who are not participants in the modeling of the system can be shown the model by running through scenarios. This can help give designers, developers, and testers a basic knowledge of the application or bring new project personnel up to speed. This technique can also be used to show customers the application. In a sense, the session can serve as a live prototype of what the system is supposed to do. And it is done in a setting in which feedback from the customers is encouraged and can be easily incorporated.

Identifying Holes in Requirements

A CRC card session provides an opportunity to literally walk through the requirements and identify holes or ambiguities. It is not uncommon during the simulation of a scenario to have someone ask, "What needs to be done next to fulfill this responsibility?" If the information in the requirements is vague, ambiguous, or missing, a domain expert needs to clarify the point. If no domain expert knows the answer, someone can commit to meet with the customer to get the answer. In either case, the author of the requirements sees the problem with the document and what needs to be done to correct it. For example, Betty noticed and vowed to change ambiguous wording in her Library requirements document.

CRC Elements at the Analysis Stage

The following discussion describes the types of classes, responsibilities, and scenarios that are unique to the problem-modeling phase of development. These are contrasted with the same CRC elements involved in design (see Chapter 5).

Classes

The classes identified in problem-modeling sessions directly reflect concepts and entities that are part of the domain being modeled. They tend to be the concepts and terms that domain experts use to describe the problem and what they want the application to do. Other classes, such as representations of implementation-level abstractions or interfaces to system resources, will be added as the system is designed (see Chapter 5). Classes at this stage are those that describe what a system does. For example, the classes we identified for the Checkbook application and the Library domain are application-level or analysis classes.

   The classes in problem modeling may include things that are outside the software system but useful in describing the way an application should behave. For example, in the Library model, the User may have been useful when describing what the system was to do but will not be useful as a software abstraction for solving the problem. Other classes in the problem model may serve as a place holder for functionality, which will be performed by more than one design class.

At the problem-modeling stage, the distinction between classes and objects may not be completely clear. Some object of the class has responsibility for doing something, but exactly which object does it and how is not completely specified. Also, dynamic issues, such as who creates an object and the lifetime of the object, are usually not dealt with until the design phase. The Library group began to get into these issues as they introduced the Collection class and wondered if objects of this class would hold Borrower and Lendable objects, but they smartly decided to defer these questions to the design phase.

Classes may also be relegated to subsystems at this stage of development. This enables parallel development from analysis through prototyping as described in Chapter 1.

Scenarios and Responsibilities

Scenarios, as discussed in Chapter 3, are detailed examples of the functioning of the system. They are the answers to questions that begin with "what happens when…" At this initial stage of development, only scenarios that explore what the system is supposed to do are considered. For example, in modeling the Library application, an important functionality of the system is to be able to check out items. Scenarios for this function included such questions as "What happens when Barbara Stewart, with one outstanding book not overdue, checks out a book, *Effective C++ Strategies?*" Most of the scenarios at this stage are driven by user-level views of the system.

Accordingly, the responsibilities that are assigned to classes during the problem-modeling CRC card sessions are of a high-level nature. Some may appear explicitly in the requirements documentation for a system. Others are derived by the group when executing the high-level scenarios. They are the steps that must take place to make the scenario happen. But they still correspond to *what* happens rather than to *how* it happens. For example, the sets of responsibilities that together describe the fulfillment of the scenario above might be the following:

- ◆ User asks Librarian to check out a book.
- ◆ Borrower checks its status.
- ◆ Book checks itself out.
- ◆ Borrower updates its set of Lendables.

But how does a Book object check itself out? The Library group decided that it updates its borrower, in or out status, and due date knowledge. Are these steps part of analysis or design? This is where things get fuzzy. Let us assume for the time being that we consider these steps to be part of the problem model. There are still lower-level considerations implicit in these steps that are unquestioningly part of design.

What does it mean for a Book to update its in or out status? Is there an attribute or data member that represents this state information that can be changed? Or does it make a change to a database table somewhere on the fly? How about Borrower's ability to borrow? We decided in Chapter 3 how Borrower determines its status via *can borrow*, but does it do so dynamically each time it is asked for it? Or does it save the status value and only recalculate if something else has changed in its state? These questions are not answered at this stage, but are deferred to design.

Later we will see how scenarios are used in CRC card design sessions to further refine the responsibilities, even to the level of member functions and their implementation. But at this stage, potentially many methods or class member function operations are collectively represented in a single piece of English text.

When Do You Have a Stable Model?

As more and more scenarios are executed in a CRC card session, the cards on the table fill out and the problem model begins to stabilize. The first sign that the model is near completion is that the execution of new scenarios, even exceptional scenarios, does not cause new classes or new responsibilities to be added to the model. Nor does executing new scenarios cause responsibilities to change classes to better handle a new situation.

The real test that a group is reaching a stable model is when a subtle shift occurs in the way the model can be used. At some point the model begins to be able to *provide* information about the problem domain rather than *require* it. It becomes a place where people are getting, rather than putting, their domain knowledge. In essence, it becomes the source of information rather than a sink for people's perceptions.

The model has become a framework for the design stage, where more information about how the system should work can be built on top of a working model of what the system does. Starting with Chapter 5, we will discuss how this design is built upon the problem model in CRC card sessions.

Library Application Problem Model

One product of problem modeling with CRC cards can be a model like the one we created in Chapter 1 for the Checkbook application. The classes and responsibilities are at a high level, corresponding to what the system is supposed to do, not how it does it. Figure 4.1 provides a picture that represents the Library application problem model. This picture, plus a set of scenarios, can be used to describe what the application will do.

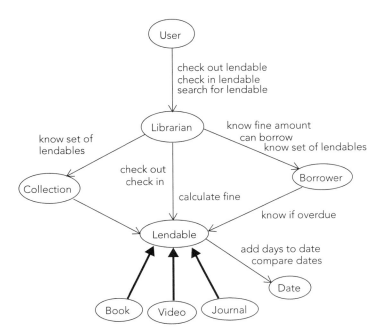

Figure 4.1 Library application problem model.

CRC Cards and Second-Generation Systems

Thus far we have presented CRC cards as a technique to build an entirely new application using an object-oriented approach. But many organizations who move to object-oriented development have an existing base of code and want to construct a second-generation system.[1] The existence of such a legacy system will undoubtedly have an impact on the development of the second-generation product. What are the choices open to these projects, and how can CRC cards support them?

Some projects jump in with both feet, rewriting the application from scratch. A more gradual approach to object-oriented development, sometimes used by projects moving from C to C++, relies on reusing some or all of the existing system. These decisions affect the project at every stage and need to be incorporated at the start of the sessions in the analysis phase. The ways in which CRC cards can be used to support these projects is explored below.

The Full-Scale Approach

If a group is considering moving to an object-oriented approach, the best business decision it can make *for the long term* is to write the new application from scratch using object-oriented techniques. This is especially true if the existing system is old or poses maintenance problems in its present form. Such a project, if the costs of training and learning are built into the schedule and the budget, can convert a group of people to object-oriented techniques while gaining the benefits advertised by the object-oriented approach. It has been suggested that the costs, over time, of not taking this full-scale approach are greater than these up-front costs.

CRC cards support this rewriting of a system much as they do the building of a new application, usually by partitioning the system and remodeling one subsystem at a time. But groups with existing systems bring additional domain knowledge into the sessions. The set of requirements for the new application drive the sessions, but are supplemented by knowledge about the existing system. Such a group also understands the strengths and weaknesses of the existing implementation, which can be an advan-

---

[1] We assume this second-generation system will be very much like the existing application with some additional features or functionality.

tage as it moves into design. This implementation-level acquaintance with the system, however, can be a disadvantage in the problem modeling of the new application because participants must separate and describe what the system does without being biased by how it currently does it.

One Subsystem at a Time

Rewriting second-generation applications using object-oriented techniques will be costly in the short term. And if the existing system is of high quality and has a healthy place in the market, abandoning it is unnecessary. However, if a portion of the system is separable from the rest, that portion can be implemented as a separate subsystem using object-oriented techniques. This may be an existing subsystem, such as the user interface, or one built to perform the new functionality required by the second-generation application.

The disadvantage of this choice is the extra work involved in bridging subsystems written using different approaches. Also, the benefits of the object-oriented approach will only apply to the one new feature. On the other hand, this hybrid approach may require training only a subset of the people on the project. It certainly allows projects to gain experience with object-oriented techniques without dedicating all the time and resources up front.

CRC cards are a popular choice to guide the analysis and design of one subsystem while training team members in the object-oriented approach. Even projects that normally use formal methodologies because of the size of their applications enjoy the informality of CRC cards for one portion of the system. System requirements that apply to the subsystem being built or rebuilt drive the scenarios. In addition to the cards to model the subsystem under consideration, the session will include a class or set of classes to hide the details of the interactions with other parts of the application. We call these classes *interface classes.*

For example, if a group wants to add a Report feature to an existing application, there may well be a Report class whose responsibilities represent the overall services that the new subsystem provides, e.g., *generate reports.* This class will collaborate with Report subsystem classes to carry out these responsibilities. In the implementation, the existing system is updated to call functions of this class to invoke the new feature. There may be other interface classes, e.g., Database or User Interface, whose responsibilities are the services of these subsystems that are required by the Report subsystem, e.g., *gather data* or *display.* The eventual implementation of these responsibilities is in terms of the code that already exists to perform these actions.

Reengineering Existing Systems

Some projects are dedicated to producing an object-based or object-oriented second-generation application but want to reuse much of the existing code. We will refer to this approach as reengineering existing systems. It is probably the least common approach of the three we mention.

This approach is much like the full-scale approach, except that the final model will necessarily be constrained by the existing system's implementation, at least at a low level. The advantages to this approach are that the resulting system will be implemented with objects, and the entire team begins to move to the new paradigm. The disadvantages are that the design, because of the constraints of the structured code, may not realize the full benefits of an object-oriented approach.

CRC card sessions to reengineer systems should build an initial object-oriented problem model and high-level design just as if the system were being rewritten from scratch. This ensures that team members gain experience in pure object-oriented analysis and design without the intrusion of the existing code.

Some analysis of the existing system should then be done. The data structures and the functions that operate upon them should be identified and grouped and CRC cards representing the resulting abstractions produced. The responsibilities on these cards are the functions that exist to operate on the enclosed data structure. These cards can then be used in the second-pass CRC card design sessions.

For example, say that in the C version of a work management system a structure called WorkTicket is central. Separate functions exist to operate on the Ticket, such as assignTicket() and closeTicket(). In sessions to reengineer such a system, a card is created to represent the Work Ticket abstraction, and it is assigned initial responsibilities, including *assign* and *close*. Later, each of the cards derived from existing abstractions are implemented as a *wrapper class*. A wrapper class is one that encapsulates the existing data structure and implements its member functions as simple calls to the functions that operate on this structure.

Reuse and CRC Cards in Problem Modeling

Reuse is not a concept unique to object-oriented development. Reuse has been a topic of exploration for years[2]. But object-oriented systems seem ideally suited to capitalize on the phenomenon. Reuse of general-purpose and special-purpose classes and frameworks is becoming widespread. Reuse of analysis classes has not happened on a large scale. But reuse of locally constructed domain classes intended for use by a particular project or family of projects within an organization is a reality.

The problem-modeling phase is not too early to begin to think about the potential for reuse in the application. Reuse of domain-level classes or architectural frameworks should be considered here. When entering a CRC card session, it is important to know what domain classes and frameworks exist to help model the problem. Then, during CRC card sessions, intelligent decisions can be made about whether the existing classes can be used for the new application. The Library application was the first such system to be written using object-oriented techniques; therefore, it could not take advantage of existing domain-level classes. But the next time a Library application is written, perhaps to support billing, purchasing, or administrative tasks, some of these cards, or sets of cards, could be reused in a problem model for the new application.

Pictures such as Figure 4.1 can be useful in identifying classes, and thus cards, in a problem model that may be reusable. Classes, or groups of classes, that have arrows only pointing in to them are good candidates for reuse because they operate independently of the other classes in the model. For example, Librarian might be the worst candidate for a stand-alone reusable component from the Library model; however, the Lendable hierarchy is a potentially good candidate to be used in another application.

CRC card sessions can also help create new domain classes or generalize existing ones to make them more reusable across applications. Cards for these classes could be stored in a card catalog for the organization. This electronic catalog could be searched for appropriate cards or sets of cards (frameworks), and copies of the cards could then be generated for the new project's use. The classes may or may not have designs and implementations associated with them. The idea of reusable problem models and how best to store, search for, and generalize the cards that represent them is an interesting area of research.

Cards as Input to a Formal Methodology

The object-oriented revolution has its roots in the programming community, where it remained for many years. Only in the mid-1980s did the use of formal methods for analysis and design move into the object-oriented arena. One reason for this is that the object-oriented approach was used mostly for small- to medium-sized applications, where formal methods have less impact. Many projects today continue to find informal techniques preferable, and CRC cards support these projects well.

When the interest in object-oriented technology moved to organizations that had used formal structured methods in the past, such as for government or defense work, object-oriented methods begin to emerge. Even for projects where size, sociology, or organization dictate the use of formal methods, CRC cards can play a part in the software development. The information gathered in sessions and stored on the cards can be the initial basis for representing a system using a formal methodology. And using CRC card sessions to generate input brings the right people together and allows a team to get a feel for the problem, and for objects, before having to learn and use a particular notation and tool.

Kinds of Methods

Formal methodologies and notations can generally be classified as either *responsibility driven* or *data driven*, depending on whether they stress behavior or data for analysis and design. Responsibility-driven approaches concentrate on class behavior to describe the what and how of a system. They view data as the support for what the classes do. Examples of responsibility-driven methods include those of Wirfs-Brock[3], Booch[4], and Jacobson [5]. Data-driven approaches concentrate primarily on the data members of classes and database tables to analyze and design the application being built. Behavior in these approaches is secondary. Examples of data-driven methods are those of Shlaer/Mellor[6,7] and, to a lesser extent, Rumbaugh[8]. CRC card output flows more naturally into notations for responsibility driven designs, but it can be useful as input to data-driven models as well.

The five methodologies described here are just a few of the almost 30 published methods for object-oriented analysis and design. These five serve as a sampling of examples of how CRC cards can provide input to different types of formal methods. Since we do not try to cover all methods, any methodology that we have omitted is left as an exercise for the reader.

The descriptions of the methodologies are cursory at best, omitting many of the details. Also, most methodologies suggest a process for object-oriented analysis and design that we do not address, concentrating instead on the notational deliverables of the method. In particular, the emphasis is on types of deliverables that can benefit most from the input of CRC cards.

Wirfs-Brock

THE METHOD

Rebecca Wirfs-Brock is the inventor of responsibility-driven design (RDD). The Wirfs-Brock methodology consists of two phases: a preliminary design phase and a final design phase. RDD is billed as a design methodology but incorporates analysis as a part of the preliminary design. The initial design phase is supported by the use of *class cards*. Each class card lists a class name, along with its responsibilities and collaborators. The cards are created and enhanced through walk-throughs of system scenarios.

The output of the preliminary design phase is then analyzed and refined to create the final design. This design is documented with a set of diagrams. Superclass and subclass relationships among classes are described in *hierarchy graphs. Collaboration graphs* describe the interactions of classes, compiled from the collaborations on the class cards. The responsibilities of each class are grouped into *contracts,* and the classes are grouped into *subsystems* to help simplify the collaboration graphs. A small subset of a collaboration graph for the Library application is shown in Figure 4.2.

Semicircle 1 in the graph refers to Borrower's contract #1, perhaps called *Provide Status Info* and consisting of the *can borrow* responsibility. In order to fulfill this responsibility, Borrower collaborates with Lendable via Lendable's contract #2. We name this contract *Is Overdue,* as it consists simply of the *know if overdue* responsibility. This is the contract or service being requested by the Borrower object in the displayed interaction. To fulfill this, Lendable will need its own contract #3, called *Know Lendable Information.* It is a grouping of Lendable's *know in or out status, know borrower,* and *know due date* responsibilities. The boxes within the Lendable box imply that Book, Video, and Journal are subclasses of Lendable.

Class descriptions are textual supplements to the model that describe each class. They list the contracts along with the constituent operations and their signatures.

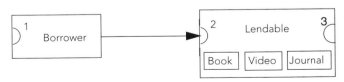

Figure 4.2 Classes in a Wirfs-Brock collaboration graph.

CRC CARDS AS INPUT

Responsibility-driven design is probably the most natural formal method to use as an extension to the CRC card technique. The RDD class card is virtually identical to a CRC card as we have described it. Wirfs-Brock describes the creation of these cards by walking through scenarios, which is exactly what is done in CRC card sessions. Therefore, the output of the sessions is the Wirfs-Brock preliminary design model.

The cards, responsibilities, collaborations, and superclass/subclass relationships identified in the sessions provide input to the second phase of RDD design. Modifications made to the RDD model during this second phase are done both off-line and in the group and should be fed back into the CRC cards for further sessions. Hierarchies formulated in the sessions are the basis for the RDD inheritance graphs. Collaboration graphs are derived by looking at the set of collaborations written on the cards, grouping the collaborating responsibilities to identify contracts, and then representing the information graphically.

Booch

THE METHOD

Grady Booch's methodology for analysis and design also concentrates on behavior, but his method includes a larger set of models and diagrams than RDD. The two main diagrams of the methodology, the *class diagram* and the *object diagram*, show relationships among classes and objects, respectively. The relationships in the class diagram are annotated to show the multiplicity of the relationship, and the form of the links denote the type of relationship. The relationships in the object diagram are labeled with the names of messages sent between the objects and can be annotated to reflect more details of the collaboration. A small class diagram and its corresponding object diagram for the Library application are shown in Figure 4.3.

Classes in the class diagram are represented as dotted "clouds."[2] The arrows denote inheritance, and the line shows a "one-to-many" has-a relationship between Borrower and Lendable. The corresponding object diagram solidifies the lines of the clouds as they become instantiated to fulfill a scenario. The arrow shows the direction of the message, and the link is labeled with the order and name of the message being passed.

---

[2]Note that the clouds are not reproduced exactly here. I suspect that the difficulty of doing so inspired their choice as an icon.

Booch's methodology also includes models such as *state transition diagrams, timing diagrams, process diagrams,* and *module diagrams.* Textual supplements include the *class template* and the *operation template.* The methodology provides a rich set of notation from which projects pick and choose as appropriate.

CRC CARDS AS INPUT

CRC cards can provide input to Booch diagrams at every phase of the life cycle to document the emerging problem model and design. Where CRC card input will be most directly useful is in formation of the class diagram and the object diagram. The information contained in these diagrams can be derived by looking at the patterns of collaboration among the cards.

The set of cards on the table, or picture (such as Figure 4.1) provided by the cards, can provide static information for the class model. Some extra thought needs to be given to the multiplicity of the relationships, but this should not be difficult for people who have been involved in the CRC card sessions. Object model input can be derived by exercising the model with the various scenarios.

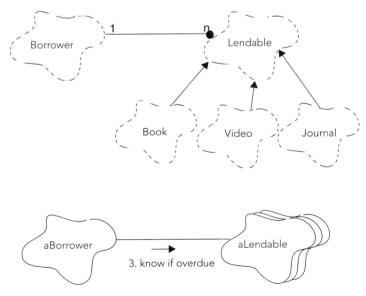

Figure 4.3 Booch class and object diagrams.

Jacobson

THE METHOD

Ivar Jacobson is the author of a methodology called Object-Oriented Software Engineering (OOSE). Developing an object-oriented application with OOSE involves building a series of models from analysis through implementation. At the core of each of these models is the notion of a *use case.* Use cases are statements that begin with "when ..." and describe uses of the system. Use cases drive the analysis by providing descriptions of what the system does and the design by providing descriptions of how it does it. Use cases can be extended and arranged in hierarchies. They are documented in *interaction diagrams* as a series of interactions among objects. A simple use case description for the Library application is shown in Figure 4.4. Steps taken in the fulfillment of the use case are listed on the left. Classes of objects that will participate in this use case are represented in the chart as vertical lines from left to right. Arrows represent interactions of objects that must take place to complete each step. The arrows are labeled with the messages sent between objects, where the message name is the responsibility of the pointed-to object.

OOSE is unique among software methodologies, concentrating less on formal notations than most. It also stresses the need for many different models for different pur-

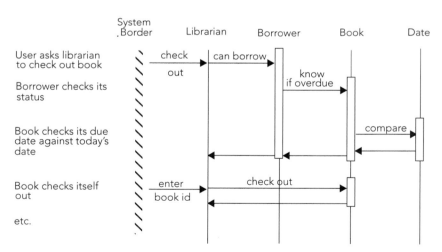

Figure 4.4 Partial OOSE interaction diagram for *check out book* use case.

poses such as interacting with customers, designers, testers, and maintainers. The accompanying software process is presented in process descriptions that focus on how the product changes throughout the life cycle. Most important to the methodology is, of course, the notion of stressing uses of the system to build reusable and adaptable applications. Use cases have been so well received that other methodologists have begun to incorporate them in their methods and notations. For example, the latest version of Booch's method includes "scripts" and object-interaction diagrams.

CRC CARDS AS INPUT

The CRC card technique maps very nicely to a formal method driven by use cases. Use cases are essentially the scenarios we use during CRC card sessions. Scenarios ask the questions, "what happens when … " How the scenarios are accomplished in the model describe the use cases. And scenario descriptions such as shown in Table 1.1 describe object interactions in a way that can be input directly to Jacobson's documentation of use cases. As we see in Figure 4.4, the parts of the use case are essentially the subtasks that have been considered in the CRC card session, and the labels on the interaction arrows are simply the responsibilities that we assigned to that object to carry out various subtasks. Since scenario descriptions are an important part of describing a CRC card model, even projects that choose not to use a formal method may decide to use the Jacobson use-case diagram as part of their documentation.

Also, the awareness of "inner" scenarios and the concept of nesting scenarios mentioned in Chapter 3 can aid the construction of hierarchies of use cases. These ideas will be discussed further in Chapter 5.

Shlaer/Mellor

THE METHOD

The Shlaer/Mellor analysis methodology relies mainly on three types of models to describe a problem. The *Information Model* is an extended entity-relationship diagram, where each object is described as a relational database table, complete with database keys. Relationships between objects are numbered, labeled with English text, and formalized using the keys. The objects in this model contain only data; no operations are mentioned at this stage. A subset of an information model for the Library application is shown in Figure 4.5.

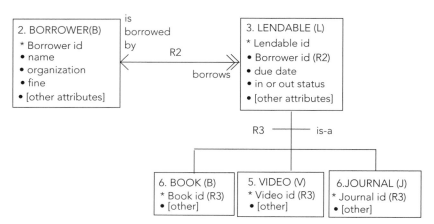

Figure 4.5 Objects in a Shlaer/Mellor Information Model.

Attributes with leading asterisks are keys, which are used in the corresponding object to formalize relationships (note the relationship number after certain attributes). All relationships are bidirectional and labeled in both directions. The multiplicity of the relationship is indicated by the number of arrows at each end. Inheritance is indicated with the "is-a" label and is based solely on data.

Textual supplements at this stage of the analysis are *object descriptions, attribute descriptions,* and *relationship descriptions.* Behavior is dealt with in the *State Model* and *Process Model* stages, wherein state diagrams of each object are drawn and operations are described via data flow diagrams.

CRC CARDS AS INPUT

The identification of the classes in a CRC card session can help build a framework for the Shlaer/Mellor information model, and the attributes from the back of the cards and *know* responsibilities can be used as a starting point for determining the data for each object. The relationship names in some cases can be determined by looking at the overall patterns of collaborations of classes, e.g., the Librarian "provides library services" to the User. In other cases, naming the relationship entails making explicit the implicit, real-world relationships that have been assumed in the sessions, e.g., Lendables "are borrowed by" the Borrower. Also, CRC card responsibilities can be used as input to the Shlaer/Mellor process models since they provide the operations to be modeled.

But CRC cards can actually have a much more important role by helping to fill what we consider to be holes in the methodology. In the Shlaer/Mellor method, the state models for each object are created, then are combined to create the *Object Communication Model* (OCM). The OCM is a picture of how all objects communicate and is similar to Wirfs-Brock's collaboration graph as well as the problem model we saw earlier in this chapter. But the state diagrams are very difficult to construct without first having some idea of how all the objects communicate. A "preliminary" OCM must be constructed before these state models are built, but the methodology provides no guidance for its construction. The model constructed as a result of CRC card sessions can be used directly as the preliminary OCM. Also, since Shlaer/Mellor allows for superclass/subclass relationships based only on data, CRC cards can be used to discover and create inheritance relationships based on behavior.

Rumbaugh

THE METHOD

James Rumbaugh's methodology, *Object Modeling Technique* (OMT), is similar to Shlaer/Mellor at a high level, but is meant for both analysis and design. The three main models of OMT capture information along the same dimensions as those in the Shlaer/Mellor method. The *Object Model* is similar to Shlaer/Mellor's Information Model but does not have the preoccupation with relational database tables and database keys. The classes in the object model also include operations as an inherent part. Various diagrams, such as the *Class Diagram*, where class relationships are described, and the *Instance Diagram*, where object relationships are documented, are parts of the object model. A subset of a Rumbaugh class diagram is shown in Figure 4.6.

In this class diagram, each class is modeled as a rectangle with three components: class name, class attributes, and class operations. The relationship between classes, such as Borrower and Lendable, is called an *association.* It is described with English text above the line. The fact that it is a one-to-many relationship is indicated by the solid circle at the end of the Lendable side of the link. Note also that the superclass/subclass relationship here is based on operations as well as data.

OMT also includes a *Dynamic Model,* which is a set of state diagrams for each object, and a *Functional Model,* where data flow diagrams describe the workings of operations. The set of relationships that can be modeled with OMT is very rich, even if you stick to the basic concepts of associations, aggregations, and generalization (inherit-

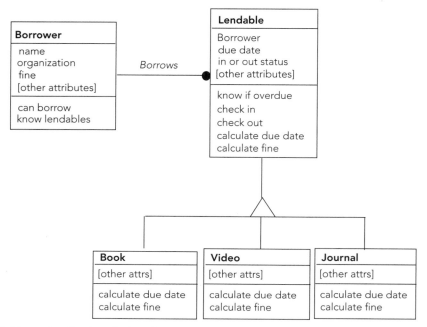

Figure 4.6 Classes in a Rumbaugh class diagram.

ance). Advanced concepts include notions such as overlapping inheritance, constraints on associations, and propagation of operations. Many different flavors of diagrams can be built. They must be chosen as appropriate, and consistency must be maintained between them.

CRC CARDS AS INPUT

CRC cards can provide input to the OMT method, mostly through the discovery of classes and class operations and class interactions. Any attributes or *know* responsibilities noted during the sessions can contribute to a description of the data in the OMT Object Model. Names and multiplicity of relationships can be discovered in sessions and input to OMT much as they are to the Shlaer/Mellor information model.

The operations, as described in the process models, are better understood by looking at the execution of scenarios in a CRC card model. And the construction of state models (as in Shlaer/Mellor) is aided by understanding the patterns of collaboration among classes. As CRC card sessions continue into design and the model mature, the progressive detail can be added to the OMT models.

Summing Up

Initial CRC card sessions concentrate on analyzing the problem domain. Classes in the problem-modeling stage are problem domain entities, and responsibilities describe what these entities do. The distribution of responsibilities is driven by scenarios that describe the use of the system from the user's point of view.

Some projects with legacy systems choose a more gradual migration to object-oriented development. CRC cards can support these projects as well as those that choose a full-scale approach. Potential reuse of domain-level classes and frameworks also needs to be explored at this phase of the project's life cycle. Some projects choose a formal methodology for creating a problem model and design. The output of CRC card sessions provides input to different formal methodologies in different ways and to different degrees. But CRC cards are always a good addition to the process because they provide a forum for exploration and discovery.

Coming Up

Many projects have never used a formal methodology to produce their systems. These projects find CRC cards to be particularly helpful in producing an object-oriented application because the cards support an informal and familiar approach while still providing a framework for implementation. Using CRC cards throughout the life cycle means that more work will be done in the implementation phase. This is because less detail will be part of a CRC card design than one produced with a formal method and notation.

Starting with Chapter 5, we will focus on the use of CRC cards through design and directly into a C++ implementation. We describe how the cards can be augmented to support the design process and how a CRC card tool can be used to capture the cards and collaborations on-line. We will also discuss some auxiliary documentation that is useful in describing a CRC card design.

References

1. *The Random House Dictionary of the English Language,* unabridged, 2nd ed. Random House Inc., New York, 1987, p. 74.

2. Tracz, Will. "Reusability Comes of Age." *IEEE Software.* 7(6):6–8 (1987).

3. Wirfs-Brock, Rebecca, Brian Wilkerson, and Laura Wiener. *Designing Object-Oriented Software.* Prentice Hall, Englewood Cliffs, NJ, 1990.

4. Booch, Grady. *Object-Oriented Analysis and Design with Applications,* 2nd ed. Benjamin-Cummings, Redwood City, CA, 1993.

5. Jacobson, Ivar, Magnus Christerson, Patrik Jonsson, and Gunnar Overgaard. *Object-Oriented Software Engineering.* Addison-Wesley, Reading, MA, 1992.

6. Shlaer, Sally, and Steven Mellor. *Object-Oriented Systems Analysis: Modeling the World in Objects.* Yourdon Press, Englewood Cliffs, NJ, 1988.

7. Shlaer, Sally and Steven Mellor. *Object Lifecycles: Modeling the World in States.* Yourdon Press, Englewood Cliffs, NJ, 1992.

8. Rumbaugh, James, Michael Blaha, William Premerlani, Frederick Eddy, and William Lorensen. *Object-Oriented Modeling and Design.* Prentice Hall, Englewood Cliffs, NJ, 1991.

CHAPTER
5

CRC Cards for Design

Analysis results need to reflect an accurate statement of the problem and

constrain possible solutions; but they don't have to work.

—Rebecca Wirfs-Brock[1]

THE MAIN DISTINCTION between the analysis and the design of an application is that the design must translate into a working program. During CRC card design sessions, additional classes and mechanisms, which support how the system works, are built upon the existing classes, which describe what the system does. While an analysis must reflect the real world of the user, the design must reflect the real world of the implementer.

In this chapter, we discuss aspects of CRC cards and sessions relating to design. We will continue our development of the Library application and see how language, environment, and efficiency considerations change and shape the model we began in Chapter 3.

We also discuss the documentation of a CRC card design and the use of CRC card tools. Finally, we provide advice on the enhancements to the cards to support the design process and facilitate the transition to implementation.

Design vs. Implementation

Just as there is some fuzziness about where analysis ends and design begins, there is also some ambiguity about when design is finished and implementation takes over. This is not a line that is clearly drawn by the use of CRC cards. Minimally, group sessions should continue until the set of necessary classes and the collaborations have been determined for a particular subsystem or set of functions. This ensures that important interactions and interfaces between classes are formulated as a group. The amount of detailed design done on each class, however, will differ from group to group.

Experienced designers may not investigate every possible scenario in design, or they may gloss over hierarchies that are similar to existing ones. The model created in the sessions becomes a framework for implementation by experienced designers and developers. On the other hand, teams new to the paradigm may want to prolong group interactions with an expert to ensure the best decisions, force peer review, and facilitate learning to the fullest.

CRC cards can be enhanced to accommodate a varying level of design detail. Because of their size, however, they cannot reflect every detailed design decision. Therefore, if a team wants to document a design to that level of specificity, it should probably record these details in another medium, perhaps even a formal notation. The discussions in this chapter and in Chapter 6 will reflect use by more experienced groups who will do some of the lowest level of design as they implement.

Strengths of CRC Cards for Design

Some of the strengths of CRC cards listed in Chapter 4 for problem modeling continue into the design stage, notably the common project vocabulary and the effective spread of domain knowledge. Additional advantages that are apparent at the design phase are discussed below.

Spreading Object-Oriented Design Expertise

Design sessions continue the process of helping participants become experienced in the object-oriented approach by showing design decisions in action. Here, choices about performance, efficiency, and other constraints are made in an object-oriented context. System and language influences are also evident. The CRC card session provides an arena for learning the design trade-offs associated with objects gradually and in a hands-on manner.

Design Reviews

Walking through scenarios in a CRC card session is an effective way to explain, or present for review, a card-based design. It can be used to bring new designers or implementers up to speed or to illustrate the workings of the system to testers. And as with the live prototyping in the analysis stage, the atmosphere is conducive to incorporating suggestions and trying alternative designs.

Framework for Implementation

Some projects have a history of doing ad hoc design as they develop. The disadvantage of this approach is that decisions about the structure of the code are not easily changed. CRC cards are a good medium for projects who have not done much design in the past to build a framework for an object-oriented implementation. Using CRC cards forces decisions to be made up front in a group setting where interactions and impacts of decisions are clear. At the same time, they are informal and flexible; thus, they do not force the developer to specify the design to an excruciating level of detail.

Informal Notation

The informality of the CRC card process allows participants to express the design in their own terms. The design emerges without being hampered by attempts to squeeze it into a notation. As Booch warns, "designing is not the act of drawing a diagram"[2]. Some object-oriented methods do a better job of teaching their notation than the tenets of the process they support. CRC cards are better than most at teaching what underlies this process and allowing designers flexibility in how they develop and document a design.

Design Constraints

As the design sessions proceed, certain real-world constraints must be considered and incorporated in the decisions made by the group. The impacts of these constraints, in such areas as environment, language, supporting software components, and performance requirements, are discussed next.

Target Environment

The first design constraint to be considered is the environment or environments in which the application will run. What machine or machines will support the application, running what operating systems? If the application is meant to run on many different machines and/or operating systems, the team will have to pay special attention to portability issues in design and implementation. The decision of environment will also have an impact on the set of supporting software components available for use.

The Library application will be running on a small network of Sun workstations running UNIX®[1] and X-Windows, with one acting as the database server. The company has always been UNIX-based, so this is a natural choice for this group. However, they are investigating PC environments and may switch to Macintosh®[2] or Windows®[3] machines sometime in the future. Therefore, the group will want to keep the UNIX-based decisions as separate as possible.

---

[1]UNIX is a registered trademark of Novell, Inc.

[2]Macintosh is a registered trademark of Apple Computer, Inc.

[3]Windows is a registered trademark of Microsoft Corporation.

Language

Much of the design of an application is independent of the particular language used for implementation. But at the lower levels, the design begins to resemble a blueprint for implementation. At this level, the set of classes that exist, and how they interact, may depend on the features of the language of choice.

The most important question about the target language as we enter the design stage is whether or not it supports object-oriented programming. If not, the design will need to do a paradigm shift at the lowest levels, and the advantages of a consistent model throughout the life cycle will be lost. Because they used C for their structured programming, the Library group migrated to C++ when they moved to development of object-oriented applications. Therefore, they have chosen C++ as the language for the Library application.

Even if the chosen language does have support for object-oriented concepts, it is important to know what feature set it supports and what software components, such as libraries and frameworks, are available for the language. For example, does the language have metaclasses, exception handling, and garbage collection? Since the Library application designers never used SmallTalk, they will not even notice that metaclasses are missing from C++. But the lack of exception handling in their version of the C++ compiler will necessitate either designing and programming an alternative or using an existing package that facilitates the handling of error conditions. Finally, the additional constraints on the use of a language imposed by the choice of a library or framework also needs to be taken into account.

Choice of Supporting Software Components

Much of the software included in a typical application today is not written by the authors of the application but provided by a third party in standard off-the-shelf packages for use or reuse by many projects. Common examples are user interface systems, database management systems, and general and special purpose libraries and frameworks. Intelligent choice of many of these software components can be made once it is known what the application is to do and what language it will use in what environment. The choice of components should be done early in design, since they will have an important impact on its final form.

USER INTERFACE

When we discuss user interfaces, we will be talking about graphical user interfaces (GUIs) and software packages that facilitate an object-oriented way of building them. Character-based interfaces are always an option, but existing character-based packages promote a structural approach to a design and do not provide the ease of use of a graphical interface. Thus, they are much less common in new applications.

Some environments provide frameworks of classes for the application interface with built-in relationships and constraints. These systems do much of the user interface work for the programmer, and they result in applications with the same look and feel. Programmers derive their own classes from framework classes, defining the implementation of certain functions and extending the implementations when necessary. These frameworks are available mainly on personal computers with graphical environments to help the user build an application. Frameworks such as MacApp on the Macintosh and the Microsoft Foundation Classes for Windows fall into this category.

Other user interface packages are written for X-Windows and are generally delivered in the form of GUI class libraries and toolkits whose objects can be extended, created, and combined in various ways by the application. Many come with packages to help build the interfaces graphically as well. FRESCO (a design evolution of the InterViews toolkit), C++/Views from Liant, Views++.h from Rogue Wave, and various libraries of X widget wrapper classes fall into this category. These packages are available on UNIX workstations. They require more design work than an application framework, and, unless a set of conventions are followed, can result in varying looks and feels.

The Library group knows that they will develop a Motif user interface but want to migrate to PCs at some point. Therefore, it is important that the GUI subsystem be kept as separate as possible. This will make it easier to move to new versions of the GUI software, or to a different system, later.

DATABASE MANAGEMENT

As design begins, the needs of the application in terms of data storage must be considered. Whether or not there is a need for persistent data will determine whether a database management system (DBMS) is a necessary part of the design. The Library team knows immediately that its application will need persistent storage; that is, there is data upon which the application depends that needs to live after the system has gone down and needs to be there the next time the system comes up. All data pertaining to the set of Lendables owned by the library as well as Borrower information will be stored in the database. Also, operations performed by the application, e.g., changes to a Book's in or out status, need to be persistently reflected in that set of data.

The choices available to projects for data management are the operating system's file system, a relational DBMS (RDBMS), and an object-oriented DBMS (OODBMS). Using files as a storage medium provides for simple interactions. Because writing to and reading from files are well-understood and simple operations, they may be a good mechanism for use as a stub when testing the main application. But since they provide no data integrity and no concurrency controls, they are not appropriate for real-world data-intensive applications.

An object-oriented DBMS is a good choice for an application in which there are complex, structured objects. An OODBMS also allows operations on data to be stored and centralized. OODBMS technology has come a long way, but is still less mature than other technologies. Relational database management systems are more mature products and are sufficient for many record-oriented applications. Many organizations have existing versions of a RDBMS, and large numbers of programmers have prior experience using them. Thus, they are a popular choice for persistent data needs.

The Library group decides on a RDBMS for the Library application. They have Oracle available and have used it extensively in the past. In order to insulate the application from their choice of a DBMS, however, they will use a special-purpose database library to interface to Oracle.

CLASS LIBRARIES

Reusing classes that are written, tested, and maintained by others is the most common type of reuse. For example, the implementation of the Borrower class in the Library application may use a general purpose C++ class, such as a parameterized List or Set, to hold its Lendables. As long as the class that is chosen is easy to use and of high quality, reusing the class will cut development, testing, and maintenance time.

The Library application needs some general-purpose libraries, as well as a library to build a Motif user interface and a library to interface to a relational database. Because they see PCs in their future, they would like to make a choice that is portable across platforms. Many general-purpose reusable libraries exist, such as the Booch Components, the Rogue Wave Library, the Microsoft Foundation Classes, the USL Standard Components, and early implementations of the standard template library from various vendors. Some of these packages are available only on UNIX platforms, and others are available only on PCs. The group decides to make a preliminary choice of the Rogue Wave libraries for their development. They contain all the components they need and are fully portable between UNIX and PCs. If other packages catch their attention before development is finished, they may consider them. But for now they will assume that they will use Views.h++ for the GUI, DB.h++ for the database interactions, and Tools.h++ for general-purpose classes.

Performance Requirements

Performance requirements are important design constraints. If the response-time performance requirements for the application are severe, the design may sacrifice some elegance and maintainability in exchange for speed. Another consideration is the expected availability of the system. That is, what hours must the application be available? If a user needs to access the system 24 hours a day, 7 days a week, then the design must include entities to insure robustness and redundancy. Finally, the requirements in terms of load are important. How many users should the application be able to handle concurrently?

The Library application requirements mandate that users receive responses to queries in less than 10 seconds, and checking in or out must take no more than 5 seconds from the time the ID of the lendable is entered. These are not very severe requirements. In terms of uptime, the Library application must be available 5 days a week from 8:00 A.M. to 5:00 P.M. each day. Maintenance, database upgrades, and data entry can thus be scheduled for the off hours. There will be only one user per system process, and the application should assume that no more than five of these processes are running at one time.

Other

Other design constraints include limits on memory usage and requirements for system security. If the memory requirements are severe, more operations will involve reading and writing to the database, even at the cost of some speed. Finally, security issues enter at the design stage. Are there limits to who can access the system? If access to the system is restricted, facilities for some kind of security or password checking need to be part of the design. Extreme security precautions may include encrypting data before it is stored on disk.

The Library application has no memory restrictions, and the data used by the Library application does not need to be encrypted; however, access to the system is limited to company employees. Therefore, use of the library will require a valid employee ID.

CRC Elements at the Design Stage

The goal of the CRC card design process is the augmentation and refinement of the classes, responsibilities, and collaborations that were determined in the problem-modeling stage. Hopefully, the refinement will be at such a level that implementation will be a fairly straightforward process (once you have read Chapter 6, that is). In this section we discuss the specifics of how CRC cards apply to design.

Classes

In Chapter 4 we decided that the classes created in analysis sessions represented entities from the problem domain. Objects of these classes collaborate in the problem model to describe what the application does. In the design phase of the CRC card sessions, classes are added that represent mechanisms that support the implementation of the problem model. Objects of these classes collaborate to describe how the problem goals will be accomplished.

Design classes reflect concepts used by designers and programmers to describe their implementation techniques. Some classes contain the data structures and operations used to implement the analysis classes. For example, our Borrower objects may contain Lists of Lendable objects. Other classes represent interfaces to hardware and software resources. The Library application will have classes that the application will use to interact with the user interface and database management subsystems.

Some rethinking of the original problem model in the face of design and implementation issues also takes place. This can result in new classes to help streamline collaborations or base classes to store common responsibilities of a set of classes. Analysis classes are sometimes found to be best implemented by a set of design classes. For instance, the responsibilities of the Collection class from analysis may be carried out by more than one new design class.

Classes to handle error conditions may be a part of the design as well. As we mentioned in the Design Constraints section, the Library application team will have to find a way to do error handling since exception handling is not implemented in their C++ compiler. The Rogue Wave Tools++.h package contains some Error-handling classes, which should be adequate for the Library application. The set of new classes that the Library team creates as they design their application is discussed in the Library Application Design section.

Scenarios and Responsibilities

Scenarios at the analysis stage are the uses of the system from the user point of view. The goal of design is to take the implementer's point of view in fulfilling these scenarios. This means detailing all system functions, including those that provide support functions, that take place as the application handles requests from the user. Since the responsibilities assigned in problem modeling describe at a high level what gets done, they are a reasonable choice to drive the scenarios for design. As the problem-modeling scenarios are repeated, the responsibilities that were assigned are detailed and fleshed out. Some tasks may need to be added, such as the ID validation when a user begins an interaction. The responsibilities already identified form a structure and order for the investigation of the details of how the system works.

During problem-modeling scenarios, the distinction between objects and classes may have been blurred, but in design, this distinction becomes important and is dealt with directly with the assignment of *create* responsibilities.

Questions such as:

♦ Who creates this object?

♦ What happens when it is created and destroyed?

♦ What is the lifetime of the object vs. the lifetime of the information held by an object?

are viable and important at this stage. How these questions are answered for classes of objects in the Library application will be an important part of its design.

As we get closer to implementation, we will need to consider C++ class questions, such as, "Do we need to define our own operations to copy and assign to objects of this class?" We leave this level of detail to the CRC-to-C++ stage of the project (see Chapter 6).

Attributes

In Chapter 3, we warned that attributes should not be assigned to classes in isolation, but only as we know they apply to the application at hand. For example, the attributes of the various kinds of Lendables were only identified and added as searching scenarios dictated. At the design stage, attributes come into play to a greater extent. The examination of each responsibility often includes the discovery of attributes necessary to support the assigned task. And it becomes clear what attributes of objects need to be saved persistently in the database. As the needs of the DBMS emerge, a database design can be created.

Knowledge of the database model is necessary before implementation can be done. It is especially necessary for the low-level design and implementation of any database interface classes. The Library database design will be done by Cecilia, the database expert, in parallel with system design. She has a preliminary model, which she will refine as information about attributes is accumulated. Her preliminary model contains tables to hold information about Borrowers, Lendables, Books, Videos, and Journals.

Enhancing CRC Card Syntax

In Chapter 4, we emphasized that the responsibilities written on a CRC card were high level and that the piece of English text describing a responsibility could encompass a number of operations. People who use 3″× 5″ index cards for the sessions should expect to record this level of responsibility.

Before the system can be implemented, many more details need to be determined about the objects and their interactions. Some of these details enter at the CRC to C++ stage, but many of the details are known during the CRC card sessions. These can be saved and represented on the cards as design scenarios are executed by the group. We will see more of this in the Library Application Design section.

This section discusses some of the enhancements that can be used in CRC card design sessions. It is best to use 4″× 6″ index cards if you plan to record the details we describe.

Subresponsibilities

In the problem modeling of the Library application in Chapter 3, we mostly listed responsibilities that reflected services required by other objects. All the responsibilities were at an aggregate level. While we discussed the steps, or subtasks, that needed to take place and the collaborations initiated to fulfill these steps, we did not explicitly record these *subresponsibilities*. This may be appropriate for describing the system at a high level, but more details are useful as a blueprint for implementation.

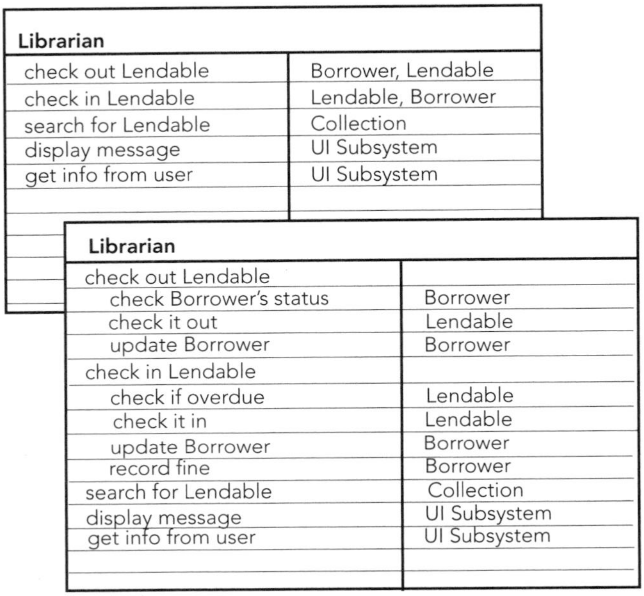

Librarian	
check out Lendable	Borrower, Lendable
check in Lendable	Lendable, Borrower
search for Lendable	Collection
display message	UI Subsystem
get info from user	UI Subsystem

Librarian	
check out Lendable	
check Borrower's status	Borrower
check it out	Lendable
update Borrower	Borrower
check in Lendable	
check if overdue	Lendable
check it in	Lendable
update Borrower	Borrower
record fine	Borrower
search for Lendable	Collection
display message	UI Subsystem
get info from user	UI Subsystem

Figure 5.1 More detailed Librarian CRC card.

For example, the Librarian had a *check out lendable* responsibility. The group discovered that in order to fulfill that responsibility, the Librarian object needed to collaborate with Borrower and Lendable objects. These collaborations were recorded on the card. But the group actually discovered that the Librarian needed to collaborate with Borrower to check its status and update its Lendable information and with Lendable to check itself out. These details were not on the card. Figure 5.1 shows the original Librarian card and a new version after more detailed subresponsibilities are listed.

Collaborating Responsibility

Another piece of information that is usually known at the time of a collaboration is the name of the collaborating responsibility. At the point in the execution of a scenario when someone points to someone else and says "I need you," it should be clear what they need from their collaborator. If the necessary responsibility does not already exist, it is created. For example, Borrower created a *can borrow* responsibility in order to give

Librarian	
check out Lendable	
check Borrower status	Borrower: can borrow
check it out	
update Borrower	Borrower: know Lend.
check in Lendable	Lendable: check out
check if overdue	Lendable: know overdue
check it in	Lendable: check in
update Borrower	Borrower: know Lend.
record fine	Borrower: know fine
search for Lendable	Collection: retrieve
display message	UI Subsystem
get info from user	UI Subsystem

Figure 5.2 Librarian CRC card with collaborating responsibilities.

status information to Librarian. Adding this responsibility to the card of the initiator of the collaboration can ease the formalization of messages later. Figure 5.2 shows the Librarian card again, this time with the collaborating responsibilities after the collaborator, separated by a colon. Notice that there are abbreviations in some places where space was tight. And everything does not line up just right. These are all advantages to an informal approach to object-oriented design. We can record what we feel we need to and in a way that we like.

Data Passed

The last enhancement that can be added to the cards is the data that is passed with the message being sent. This usually takes place just at the end of the design phase, as a prelude to a translation to code. For the Library application, we will incorporate this as part of the translation to C++. But it can be added any time the designers know the information and want to record it. Groups that take design to a low level will save this information, although they sometimes switch to another documentation medium, rather than save it all on the card.

Figure 5.3 shows the Librarian card with some of the message data noted on it. You can begin to see how the notation is looking more like code. Also, notice that the information is more in the form of notes to the implementer than a formal specification. For example, the data passed is sometimes expressed as a type, e.g., "Lendable," sometimes as an attribute, e.g., "fine," and sometimes as groups of attributes, e.g., "info."

Librarian	
check out Lendable	
check Borrower	Borrower: can borrow
check it out	Lendable: check out(Borr)
update Borrower	Borrower: know Lend.(Lend)
check in Lendable	
check if overdue	Lendable: know if overdue
check it in	Lendable: check in
update Borrower	Borrower: know Lend.(Lend)
record fine	Borrower: know fine(fine)
search for Lendable	Collection: retrieve(info)
display message	*UI Subsystem*
get info from user	*UI Subsystem*

Figure 5.3 Librarian CRC card with some data added.

Library Application Design

Once the Library application group feels they have agreed on a stable model of what the application should do, the sessions shift to the design of the system that will do it. Cecilia and Jim, the designers and developers, become the prominent members of the team. Betty remains as a participant to ensure that design decisions do not violate the analysis model. Nancy remains as the facilitator to continue to guide the object-oriented design. Betty inherits Dewey's Collection class card for the execution of scenarios, and Jim takes the Date class card.

Nancy tells the group not to worry if the resulting design is structurally different from the problem model. She suspects that many of the classes will remain but that responsibilities and collaborations will change and new classes will be added. Betty also adds that she expects that new considerations such as language and machine will alter the design model. But she, along with the previously built problem model, is there to keep them honest in terms of what the system should accomplish.

Nancy prepares the design team for more detailed scenario execution by explaining how the cards can be enhanced (see section on CRC Card Enhancements). The group tries it out on the Librarian card for practice. Jim and Cecilia like the idea of adding sub-responsibilities to the cards. They may add some collaborating responsibilities when it does not interrupt the flow but think that the data will be less useful at this stage.

As the group delves into design, they ask Nancy for an order in which to address items. She states that, as usual, there is no prescribed order and the group should do what feels right for them. The core of the session should be, as in problem modeling, executing scenarios, this time to a lower level of detail. But perhaps they should begin, as they did in problem modeling, by brainstorming any new classes that spring to mind.

Classes

Jim claims that he will feel more comfortable if they specify to a greater extent the role and operations of the classes that serve as interfaces to other subsystems, even at a high level. More detailed responsibilities can be added as the scenarios are executed. This will give him a framework for communication with other subsystems and is essential for partitioning of the prototyping work. The group chooses to tackle that first.

USER INTERFACE

The team has already decided that it wants to keep the GUI subsystem as separate as possible. To achieve this goal, Jim suggests a class named UI Manager to serve as a layer of insulation between the application and the actual GUI system of classes. It will have Library-specific responsibilities, which it carries out by collaborating with the GUI subsystem classes.

Cecilia interrupts with an issue. She likes the idea of the class, but notes that she read somewhere that "Manager" classes are a bad idea in object-oriented design. So she feels somewhat uncomfortable with the choice of name.

Nancy agrees that the literature sometimes warns against "Manager" classes. This is not a widely accepted taboo, but those that do not like the word think that more precise names can usually be found to describe the class, e.g., Process Scheduler rather than Process Manager. She thinks that if "Manager" describes their vision of the class precisely, they should use it. If not, they should come up with a more descriptive name. Would UI Request Broker or UI Request Dispatcher be better? Cecilia thinks that "UI" refers more to how it carries out its responsibilities, not what it does. It is really just a User Interacter. Is that too silly a name? The group decides that it will work for the time being.

So how does the User Interacter fit into the design of the system? Jim draws his view of the position of the User Interacter in the system in a diagram that looks like Figure 5.4. At a high level, the User Interacter is responsible for obtaining specific types of information from and displaying information to the users of the application. It uses GUI subsystem objects, such as Menus, Dialog Boxes, and Views, to interact with users.

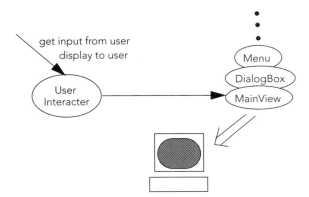

Figure 5.4 User Interacter class interface to GUI software.

Betty is puzzled about the User Interacter class. She admits knowing little about design, but knows that in the real world the Librarian *is* the user interacter. Couldn't Librarian be used to insulate the application from the user interface? Nancy explains that the Librarian will interact with the user, but will do so with the help of the User Interacter class so that it does not have to rely on a specific GUI system. Interfacing to specific pieces of code is really an implementation-level task. Assigning such low-level tasks to problem model classes is probably not a good idea.

Cecilia offers to take the User Interacter card, since she named it. She is also the group expert on user interfaces.

DATABASE

The team turns their attention to the database management subsystem. They discuss the need for a new class to insulate the application from DBMS-specific calls. Jim suggests that Collection could serve that purpose. It already collaborates with the database (DB) subsystem in the problem model. Do they really need another layer? Cecilia reminds the group that Collection was chosen to represent a different abstraction: the Collection of Lendables in the Library. They need a new implementation-level class to simply interface with the DBMS, especially since they also need to obtain and store Borrower objects as well as objects of each of the Lendable classes.

Cecilia points out that the Rogue Wave DB++ classes provide some insulation from the DBMS; perhaps they don't need an additional class simply for this purpose. But Jim

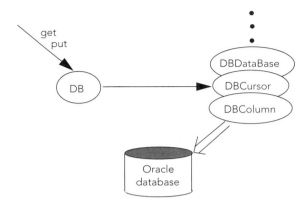

Figure 5.5 DB class interface to data management software.

claims that the insulation is not deep enough for a clean switch to a totally different kind of data management, such as an OODBMS. They might even want to use the file system instead of a database management system as a stub to test the Library code. With another class just to do database interactions, the real implementation in terms of DB++ classes could be swapped in later.

Nancy agrees with Jim but shares Cecilia's concern about using the name Collection for this class. In addition to the fact that it refers to a different concept in the problem model, Collection is a common term for a generic class that holds other objects. How about creating a class that more directly reflects an interface to the DBMS? Cecilia then proposes that they simply create a DB class, and the team agrees. Cecilia volunteers for this card since, as the database expert, she will be responsible for its implementation. She draws Figure 5.5 on the board to clarify DB's place in the system. The team now feels comfortable with the set of classes and decides to begin scenario execution.

Responsibilities and Scenarios

As the team begins scenario execution, the following cards are in play with the following owners. Betty owns Librarian and Collection. Jim owns the Lendable hierarchy, with lendable, Book, Video, and Journal. He also has the Date class. And Cecilia owns Borrower, User Interacter, and DB.

CREATION SCENARIOS

Jim points out that in the problem model, the group was not very cognizant of objects being created and destroyed; and they need to pay more attention to that now. Nancy agrees that this distinction between class and object will be important in the design phase. She suggests that they consider the following questions as they deal with objects in the scenarios.

1. What is the lifetime of the object?

2. Who is responsible for creating/destroying the object?

3. What happens when it is created and destroyed?

Jim starts thinking out loud about the lifetime of objects. He hypothesizes that some classes, such as interface classes, will most likely have just one object in the system which is alive the entire time that the process is running (from 8 to 5 each day). Other objects, such as Borrowers and different kinds of Lendable objects, will be created and destroyed much more dynamically. Some Lendable objects, for instance, will only survive through one transaction (the time in which the Librarian answers a particular request, e.g., check in, check out, or search). And most Borrower objects will be created for the length of session (or a series of transactions for a particular user) and destroyed when the session is finished.

While they are on the subject, Cecilia wants to clarify the interactions with the database for the objects that are very dynamic in the system (objects of type Book, Video, Journal, and Borrower). What happens when an object of this type is created and destroyed? She thinks that if they do create scenarios for these objects now, it may simplify the subsequent scenario execution.

For instance, when a user enters his or her ID into the system, the Librarian needs to get a Borrower object that corresponds to that user. Does Librarian create it, or does it get the Borrower object from the DB? Jim likes the former model. He thinks Librarian will access Borrower's create responsibility, passing the ID that the employee enters.

Figure 5.6 Jim's perception of the creation of a Borrower.

Then he sees the Borrower interacting with the database through DB to find the right information in the database to populate its state. He draws Figure 5.6 on the board to illustrate. Cecilia disagrees. She sees DB as saving and retrieving objects, not pieces of information. If that is true, then Librarian gets a new Borrower object from DB when it is given the employee ID. The DB collaborates with the DB++ classes to get the necessary data to create a Borrower. She sketches Figure 5.7 on the board to illustrate her viewpoint.

They seem to be at an impasse, so they turn to Nancy for help. Nancy's concern about Jim's approach has to do with the eventual implementation in C++. If the Borrower's constructor (the C++ implementation of the create responsibility) gets information from the database to populate itself, then the destructor must store that information, through DB, to the database. But constructors and destructors in C++ are sometimes called when the programmer isn't even aware of it. For example, a copy constructor (which may actually be created by the compiler) is called when argument objects are passed to functions, and constructors and destructors are called to support the creation and destruction of temporaries. Creating a new Borrower from an existing one clearly does not necessitate a visit to the database, so the destruction of such an object should not require one either. Given that there is only one destructor defined per class, it is better if it does not access the database.

Alternatively, Borrower could have some sort of initialization responsibility, separate from the constructor, which asks DB for information. But Nancy thinks it would be cleaner if DB supported explicit operations to get or store objects from the database. That was why they added the extra level in the first place. Getting and putting objects from and to a DB mimics the operations of an OODBMS more closely, which will make it easier if they ever decide to migrate in that direction.

Jim recognizes that as fairly clear advice; so they decide on Cecilia's model. Cecilia adds *get Borrower, put Borrower,* and *create Borrower* as operations of DB. Since the discussion will hold just as well for Books, Videos and Journals, she also adds *get Lendable, put Lendable,* and *create Lendable* to the DB card.

Figure 5.7 Cecilia's perception of the creation of a Borrower.

Nancy suggests that the group do a new, very simple scenario: "What happens when the system is started up each day?" Cecilia jumps in.

> **DB**: Well, as Jim said earlier, one instance should suffice as an interface to the database management system. So as that object, I must be created at system start up. My lifetime will be for the life of the entire process. I guess I am created by the Library application itself, implemented as the C++ main() routine. What happens when I am created?

Jim thinks they should consider two scenarios here. The DB object could establish a connection to the DBMS as it is created, which is closed when the object is destroyed. Then read and update operations could just use this open connection. Otherwise, connections could be opened and closed each time a read or update operation is performed. The first model is certainly the simplest and most efficient, but he is concerned that, with multiple Library application processes accessing the DBMS, they could run out of connections. Betty reminds the team that the requirements specify that the application need support no more than five concurrent processes, which should be well under the limit for DBMS connections. The team agrees and thus settles on the first model of DB creation.

> **DB:** So I add a *create* responsibility to my card and write DB++ classes as my collaborator to help create the connection. Okay, now I am done. Who's next?
>
> **User Interacter:** Well, as another interface class object, I probably get created now. But I can't think of anything significant that happens when I am created. So I won't even write a *create* responsibility. I'm done.
>
> **Librarian:** I'll be next. I can't think of much that happens as I am created. But soon afterwards I must become ready to handle user requests. So the library application must send me a message to sit and wait for people to come in and ask for help. Therefore, I am going to add a responsibility to *wait for user*. I probably collaborate with User Interacter to do this, since it has the responsibility to get an employee ID from a user.
>
> **User Interacter**: That's true. I will add *get employee ID* as a responsibility.

The group decides that this is about all they can classify as system start-up. Anything further requires a user-level scenario. So they move on to one of those.

CHECK-OUT SCENARIO

Nancy suggests that the team next do a simple check-out scenario and attempt to fill in details of the design. Jim would like to see all the gory details, even if some of the responsibilities already exist. They can short-cut on later scenarios. Nancy suggests doing the first scenario on their list: "What happens when Barbara Stewart, who has no fine and one outstanding book, not overdue, checks out a book entitled *Effective C++ Strategies*?"

> **Librarian**: Okay, I guess the ball is in my court, since I am sitting waiting for a user to log in. I will collaborate with User Interacter to get the User's ID, using its *get employee ID* responsibility.

> **User Interacter**: Right. I will carry this out by collaborating with some Views.h++ classes. It will be some kind of form in the main Library view in which the user will enter the ID.

Cecilia mentions something that occurred to her as Jim talked about lifetime classifications. Librarian can perform numerous transactions for a particular user; therefore, it seems to her, the Librarian object should have some notion of a current borrower. The team agrees, so Betty adds *know current borrower* to her list of responsibilities as Librarian and continues the scenario.

> **Librarian**: When Barbara enters her ID, I will collaborate with DB to get the Borrower object for Barbara Stewart, which becomes my current borrower.

Cecilia breaks in again, reminding Betty that the ID that is entered needs to be verified for security reasons. They will probably need some object to do this verification. Betty wonders if they really need a class to do that, or will that just be Librarian's responsibility.

Nancy enters here with an important point. A class to do verification may seem very simple, and so there is a temptation to just have the Librarian take this responsibility. After all, it will have to initiate this verification anyway. But giving Librarian the knowledge and responsibility to carry out the verification is very different from having it ask someone else to do it. The goal of object-oriented design is to share the knowledge and behavior necessary to do a task. By having a separate class who knows about employee IDs and checking for matching entries, Librarian is spared the responsibility for this knowledge.

The team decides that it is better to protect Librarian from these details and creates a class called ID Verifier. Jim volunteers to take this class for the scenario execution.

> **Librarian**: Okay, let's back up a step. Before I get a Borrower object, I *verify the employee ID*. To do this, I collaborate with ID Verifier.

> **ID Verifier**: I must have a *verify* responsibility. I probably look in the current employee database table. Cecilia, you should probably add an Employee table to the database model. Anyway, Librarian, I found Barbara.

> **Librarian**: Good. Now I can get a Borrower object using the employee ID.

By the way, asks Jim, what kind of a thing is the employee ID and the Lendable ID, for that matter? Do we need a class to represent them? Betty says that the ID is just a string of characters and numbers. So the team decides to represent IDs with a reusable String class.

Librarian: I pick up here still holding my card up and still collaborating with DB to get the Borrower object for Barbara Stewart.

DB: I use my *get Borrower* responsibility, in which I *get data from the DBMS* and then use it to *create Borrower*, collaborating with Borrower, of course.

Borrower: As I create myself, I need to create my set of previously borrowed Lendable objects. Perhaps I will just create an empty set and let DB give me the actual Lendables to put on it.

DB: The Borrower table in the database will have the IDs for the lendables. So, I use these IDs and my *get Lendable* responsibility (in which I *get data from the DBMS*) to *create Lendable*. Actually, I create a Book object in this case, which I can give to Borrower to add to her set.

Borrower: Using my *know set of lendables* responsibility, of course.

Cecilia notes that in order to construct her set, she will collaborate with whatever it is that actually holds her Lendables. By the way, what kind of data structure should this be? Should it be an array, a linked list, or a set class? She needs to delete things from the middle, so an array is probably not a good idea. She needs to search it; but since it will never be more than five elements, this shouldn't really be a performance problem. She does not need any set operations, and Set classes are usually more complicated than List classes. Cecilia decides she will use a simple, singly linked list. When she checks the documentation for Tools.h++, she notes that there are numerous choices of List classes. They all have the basic behavior she needs, such as retrieving items, adding and deleting items, and knowing how many items are on the List. For now, she will write down List as her collaborator and decide during prototyping the exact type to use.

Borrower: I have a *know set of lendables* responsibility, which implies maintenance of this set. I will split these into *add lendable to set*, *delete lendable from set*, *retrieve lendable from set*, and *number of lendables*. List will be my collaborator for all of these.

DB: I will use Borrower's *add lendable to set* responsibility for each of the Lendables; actually, in this case, there is just one previously borrowed book. Then I can give the Borrower object to Librarian and she can continue the scenario.

Librarian: Great! Now I am the only one in the air again. Next I need to get a choice of transaction from the user, and then do what they ask. I must use User Interacter to get the choice from the user.

User Interacter: I will add a *get user action* responsibility. And I will use GUI classes, probably a Menu, to obtain this information. Okay, Librarian, the user chose "check out."

Librarian: Then I will execute my *check out lendable* responsibility. First I need to *check borrower status* to see if she is allowed to borrow something. We added that subresponsibility earlier. I collaborate with Borrower to do this.

Borrower: So I get into the picture again with my *can borrow* responsibility. I guess we need to detail what this means. First, I check my fine (with my *know fine amount* responsibility) to see if it exceeds $100. Nope, my fine is at $0. I have a set of lendables. I use my *number of lendables* responsibility (collaborating with List) to discover that there is one book in the set, so I am not over my lendable limit. Now I need to find out if it is overdue. I guess this will be a subresponsibility. I collaborate with List to *retrieve lendable from set*, and I collaborate with that Book object to see if it is overdue.

Book: Right. I have my *know if overdue* responsibility to handle this request. Time out, do I have an overdue attribute, or do I figure it out each time?

Jim is asking a typical question about the retrieval of a component of an object's state. Is there an attribute that stores this information and is retrieved? Or is the value calculated from other attributes each time it is created? Cecilia believes that a Lendable should just calculate whether or not it is overdue each time. Jim agrees, stating that it is not a very expensive operation.

Book: So to calculate this, I need to compare my due date with today's date. So I need to collaborate with Date for this. By the way, where did today's date come from?

Nancy suggests that Jim (in his role as Date) has a responsibility to know today's date, so he writes *know today's date* on his Date card.

Book: Okay, back to the scenario. Date, compare these dates.

Date: I'll use my *compare dates* responsibility for this. I will probably implement this using Date's operator<() in the C++ code. Then Book can just ask if due date is less than today. For this scenario, it is.

Book. Good. Then I am not overdue, Borrower.

Borrower: Okay, then, Librarian. That was my only Lendable; so I can borrow. Back to you.

Librarian: Since the Borrower status is okay, I need to ask the Lendable to check itself out. Wait, I don't have a Lendable; I need to know what lendable she is checking out. I guess I ask User Interacter to find this out for me.

User Interacter: I will *get lendable ID* from the user for you. I'll probably use some kind of form in which the User will type the ID.

Librarian: Now I need to get the actual Lendable from the DB object, using that ID.

DB: We've just been through my *get Lendable* responsibility in detail, so let's not do that again. Let's just say I give you the Book object.

Librarian: Fine with me. I guess if you couldn't find a matching Lendable, I should display an error message. That's really an exceptional scenario. In this scenario, I get an OK, then ask the new Book object to check itself out. Book?

Book: Got it. I have a *check out* responsibility. This simply entails setting my borrower attribute, setting my in or out status to OUT and calculating my due date. I guess I need Date to help me do this, because I have to add 28 days to the current date.

Date: Yep. I have an *add days to date* responsibility (operator+(int)) in C++ lingo). Done.

Book: Then I guess I'm done checking out.

Librarian: Now the check-out is done. No, I forgot. I've got to tell Borrower to update its list of lendables then ask DB to store the Book object. Borrower?

Borrower: I will add the Book object to my set using my *add lendable to set* responsibility collaborating with List. But rather than asking DB to store this Book now, why not just let DB store all my lendables later when it stores me in the database?

Jim wonders if that will really work. What if the Borrower wants to check the book right back in? It won't be updated in the database. Cecilia claims that it should work as long as they adopt a model where Librarian gets the Lendable object from the Borrower (rather than the database) when checking it in. Nancy suggests they go with this design for the time being and do a return scenario next to verify that it works.

Librarian: Then I guess this transaction is finished and I wait for the next request from Barbara. As before, I collaborate with User Interacter to get the next request. Let's not go through that in detail. We know I will get an "exit" request back, and then the session is finished. Finally, I give my current Borrower back to DB.

DB: And I store the Borrower data via my *put Borrower* responsibility and the DB++ classes. And I guess we decided that I store the Lendable data from the set via my *put Lendable* responsibility. Then I destroy the Borrower object and each of its Lendable objects.

Borrower: I'm gone.

Librarian: I guess I'll just sit here and wait for the next user to arrive. (Maybe I'll have time to get some coffee :-)

RETURN SCENARIOS

Cecilia is eager to do a check in scenario next. After examining the new Librarian card, she thinks she has an idea for simplifying the interactions there. So the group decides to do a detailed walk-through of the first return scenario on their list: "What happens when Liz Flanagan returns her book, *Barely Managing O-O Projects*, on time?"

Librarian: Well, I again need to *wait for user* to log in. I will get an employee's ID with the help of User Interacter and verify its validity by collaborating with ID Verifier. We went through that before, so we know how that works. I do many of the same things I do for the check out scenario. So we don't need to go through these in detail. Why don't we just wave cards as I list what needs to be done? First, I set my current borrower by getting the Borrower object from DB.

DB: Here you go.

Librarian: Got it. Next, I will collaborate with User Interacter to get the user's choice of what to do.

User Interacter: It's "check in" this time.

Librarian: Okay. So I again collaborate with User Interacter to get the Lendable ID (just wave that User Interacter card, Cecilia). But this time I get a Lendable by collaborating with Borrower.

Borrower: Right. Maybe I can use my *retrieve lendable from set* responsibility.

Librarian: So here is where things start to diverge from the last scenario. I ask the Book object if it is overdue, so I know whether to assign a fine to the Borrower.

Book: And we went through how I fulfill my *know if overdue* responsibility in the last scenario also. I collaborate with Date and discover that I am not overdue.

Librarian: Good, now check yourself in!

Wait, says Cecilia. This is where I have a problem. Couldn't Book check whether or not is was overdue while it was checking itself in? This would cause less bouncing back and forth and one less interaction between Librarian and Book. Betty admits that it sounds good, but wonders how Librarian will know the amount of the fine to charge Borrower if Book does the overdue check. Jim, who likes the new idea, suggests that Librarian could start by asking Book to check itself in, rather than asking if it is overdue. Then Book's *check-in* responsibility could return to Librarian the amount of the fine as follows:

Book: In this case I am not overdue, so my fine amount is zero. Otherwise, I would have executed *calculate fine* to figure it out. In fact, it may be more efficient to just calculate the fine to return. I'll figure this out when I implement it. Anyway, I check myself in; that is, I change my in or out status to IN and clear my borrower and due date attributes. Then I return the fine amount to you, Librarian.

Librarian: And since there is no fine in this case, I don't have to update the Borrower's fine amount. (But if there was, I would. And I would display a message to Liz about it as well.) But in this case, I can go ahead and tell Borrower to update its set of Lendables.

Nancy stops the scenario execution this time, saying that something just occurred to her. She wonders what would happen if the user checking in the book were not the same as the user who borrowed the book? Is that allowed in this application, or should that be an error? Jim says that he doesn't think that should be an error, but Cecilia suggests that allowing a user to return another borrower's material will just complicate things, and it will be much simpler to just not allow it.

Betty speaks up at this point. This is a question of what the application should do. It should not be decided based on what is easiest to implement. She's right, of course, and everyone knows it. Nancy asks her if this behavior will be allowed in the application, and she says that it will.

This implies that the Book itself is the only one that really knows who took it out. So the Book has to tell someone who the real borrower is. Cecilia reminds the group that they don't have a Book to ask anything if they have the wrong Borrower, because they got the book from the Borrower in the first place. Everyone is tired and frustrated. Nancy suggests that they quit for the day, mull over alternatives, and meet the next day refreshed.

The group arrives the next morning with some new ideas. Cecilia begins by suggesting a new responsibility for DB as a solution to their current dilemma. Librarian first checks for the book (given the Lendable ID) on Borrower's set. Betty can add a subresponsibility to do this. If the Book, in this case, is not there, Librarian can ask DB to get a new Borrower object *given the lendable ID*. The database should have the information to get a Borrower object by either employee ID or lendable ID. Couldn't *get Borrower* just be an overloaded function in the implementation? Jim likes the general outline of the idea. Betty remarks that it is fine with her, but she just ran out of space on her Librarian card and is feeling a little overloaded herself.

Jim remarks that this is where his idea can help. Ever since he mentioned a transaction before, he has been wondering if they should create classes to represent transactions. He thinks that this might resolve some of their present concerns. They could create Check Out and Check In classes and group the common state and behavior into a Transaction superclass. Librarian could create Check In and Check Out objects that would be responsible for interacting with the correct Borrower. This would off-load some of Librarian's interactions.

The team decides to redo the current scenario using this approach, starting at the point where Librarian gets the "check in" choice from User Interacter. Betty takes a new card for Librarian, since she will give away some of her responsibilities, and Jim takes the Transaction hierarchy.

Librarian: Instead of executing a *check in lendable* responsibility, I will add a *create and execute transaction* responsibility with Transaction as my collaborator. In this case, I will actually create a Check In object. I pass my Borrower object with this collaboration, since Check In will need to have a Borrower to work with. I guess I will let it get the Lendable objects, so I get rid of that subresponsibility as well. I will still get the lendable ID from the user, with User Interacter's help, and pass that along too.

User Interacter: There you go.

Librarian: Thanks, now I will rip in half the old Librarian card and put it on the discard pile. Check In?

Check In: When I am created, I will set my Borrower to that given me by Librarian (via a *know current borrower* I just added). Then I will get the matching Lendable from my current Borrower to set my current Lendable (I'd better add *know current lendable* to my card), collaborating with Borrower, of course.

Borrower: Here it is, I got it with my trusty *retrieve lendable from set* responsibility.

Cecilia pauses to point out that if Check In can't find the Lendable object in the Borrower's set, it will get a new Borrower from DB. So Check In should actually list DB as a collaborator for *create* as well as Borrower. True, says Nancy. But in this scenario, Liz is the same Borrower who originally checked out *Barely Managing O-O Projects*.

Librarian: Now I will ask the Check-In object to execute.

Check In: I will add *execute* to all of my Transaction cards. As part of my *execute* responsibility, I ask the Book to check itself in.

Book: I check to see if I am overdue, then change my internals to reflect the fact that I am IN. Done. And I return the fine amount.

Check In: I guess I inherited the fine-related responsibilities from Librarian also. So I ask Borrower to update it's list by taking the book off and update its fine amount.

Betty breaks in this time. She has a concern about the fine. All they have considered in design is the total amount of the fine for a given borrower. Any program that prints bills needs to print the name of the lendable as well as the fine amount. In fact, the bill should also contain the due date and the date returned. She realizes that another application will actually print the bills, but this application needs to provide the correct information.

Jim agrees, but notes that Borrower simply needs to know its total fine so that it can determine its borrowing status. He suggests that Borrower should continue to just save that knowledge. He also thinks that they should add a class called Fine that associates a Lendable with a fine amount and important dates. Objects of this class could be created and stored in the database in a Fine table by Check In as part of its *execute* responsibility.

Cecilia argues that Check In could actually ask DB to write the information to the database without the existence of a Fine class. Jim agrees but thinks it is better to have a separate class to group the information than have DB have detailed knowledge of fine information. Then Check In can give DB a Fine object to store, which is consistent with the rest of the model. Besides, he has already created the card and has started writing attributes on the back. The team decides to add a Fine class to the design as Cecilia adds *put Fine* to her DB card. She also makes a note to add a Fine table to the database design, which will be used more extensively in other applications for printing overdue notices. Nancy asks if anyone remembers where they were.

Borrower: I remember where we are because I am still holding this card up! I was just asked by Check In to update my set by taking the book off and update my fine amount. I don't have a fine in this case. But while I'm thinking about it, I will change my responsibility to *know total fine amount*. I also have a *delete lendable from set* responsibility, which I will use to update my set, collaborating with List. Then I am done.

Check In: So it is time for me to make my departure. I will record this as a *destroy* responsibility on my card. I will list DB as a collaborator since I give my Lendable to DB (and the new Borrower if I needed to get one, Cecilia).

DB: Thanks, the new Book record is safely stored in the database.

Check In: Good. Now I'm history.

Librarian: The rest of the scenario is the same as the last one. I get an "exit" request using User Interacter, store my Borrower via DB, and then sit and wait for the next session to begin.

The team likes the new design, so they redo the check-out scenario to see if it holds up. In that scenario, Librarian creates and executes a Check Out object instead of executing a *check out lendable* responsibility. The Check Out object checks the Borrower status, so Librarian loses that subresponsibility also. The Library design team is happy with this current set of classes and division of labor.

The updated set of cards is shown below.

User Interacter

get employee ID	Views.h++ classes
get user action	Views.h++ classes
get lendable ID	Views.h++ classes
display message	Views.h++ classes
display ok or cancel message	Views.h++ classes

DB

create	DB++ classes
get information from DBMS	DB++ classes
get Lendable	Lendable
get Borrower	Borrower, Lendable
put Lendable	Lendable

put Borrower	Borrower
put Fine	DB++ classes

Librarian

wait for user	
get and verify employee ID	User Interacter, ID Verifier
know current borrower	DB
create and execute transaction	User Interacter, Transaction
get lendable ID	User Interacter
display error messages	User Interacter

ID Verifier

verify	DB++ classes

Transaction

subclasses: Check In, Check Out

create	
know current borrower	
execute	

Check Out

create	
know current borrower	
know current lendable	DB
execute	
check borrower status	Borrower
check out lendable	Lendable
update borrower	Borrower
display errors	User Interacter
destroy	
put lendable	DB

Check In

create	
know current borrower	
know current lendable	Borrower
get alternate lendable	DB
execute	
display errors	User Interacter

check in lendable	Lendable
create and store Fine	Fine, DB
update borrower	Borrower
destroy	
put borrower	DB
put lendable	DB

Fine

know borrower
know lendable
know fine amount
know due date
know returned date

Borrower

create	List
can borrow	
know total fine amount	
know number of lendables	List
retrieve lendable from set	List
check overdue lendable	Lendable
add lendable to set	List
delete lendable from set	List

Lendable

subclasses: Book, Video, Journal

calculate due date	Date
calculate fine	Date
check out	Date
check in	
know if overdue	Date
know due date	
know borrower	
know in or out status	

Book

superclass: Lendable

calculate due date	Date
calculate fine	

Video	
superclass: Lendable	
calculate due date	Date
calculate fine	

Journal	
superclass: Lendable	
calculate due date	Date
calculate fine	

Date	
know today's date	
compare dates	Date
add days to date	

SEARCH SCENARIO

Next, the group bravely launches into a search scenario to see if their new design can be extended to accommodate this functionality. Betty suggests that a search is probably just another Transaction. Cecilia questions this, saying that searching is simply querying the data base and displaying information and has nothing in common with the other transactions. But Betty claims that Check In and Check Out really have little in common besides the fact that they are executed; and a Search is executed as well. In the problem domain, they are all Transactions. For description purposes, she likes the idea of a complete Transaction hierarchy.

Jim likes it too. It fits nicely into the present model by simply creating a subclass and defining its *execute* responsibility. He suggests that a Search could replace Collection in the problem model. After all, they did decide earlier that Collection is not a good name for a class. Librarian could create and execute a Search object, and it can be responsible for collecting the necessary information from the user (through User Interacter), getting the data from database, using DB, and displaying it, with User Interacter's help again. This is consistent with Check In and Check Out.

The team agrees to try this approach; and Jim grabs a card as Betty rips her Collection card in two and begins the search scenario, "What happens when Ned Brooks comes to the Library in search of a book entitled *The Mythical Mammoth?*"

Librarian: Okay, I get a "search" choice from User Interacter. I guess I create a Search object and then execute it.

Search: I take over with my *execute* responsibility. I must do things like find out what the user is looking for. Then display a form for the user to fill out. Then I use DB to get matching Lendables based upon what is entered in the form. It sounds like I just collaborate with User Interacter and DB to generate forms to collect information and then to display the result to the user. This is pretty simple.

Cecilia agrees with Jim that this is what takes place at a high level. But there are implications for new DB responsibilities to get objects from the database based on different sets of information. And this is where the attributes of the Lendables become important again, because they are the fields that the user will key on to locate a particular book, video, or journal.

Search: Okay, let's think about what I need the User Interacter to get me. First, I need to know what type of Lendable I am searching for. User Interacter, find out what kind of thing the user is looking for; then I can ask you to display the right form to collect the information.

User Interacter: Why don't I just *collect search info*? As part of this responsibility I can ask the user the type of Lendable and display the correct form based on the answer. You don't need to get involved at every step.

Search: Okay with me, so get me the search information.

User Interacter: For this scenario, we are looking for a book. What should the user be able to search on? Let's give them a form to fill in title and/or author. I will collect the information and give it to you, Search.

Search: Then I take the information and ask DB to give me the matching book.

DB: Actually, there might be more than one book that matches. So I think I should return a list of Books to you. In the meantime, I need to do some more sophisticated searching of the database. I can do that (with my *get information from dbms* responsibility) and I can already *create Lendable* objects. So I guess I just return the list to you. By the way, what did Ned enter?

Nancy suggests that their scenario is not specific enough. They need to specify what information the user entered and what the DB found. Let us assume that the user enters "Ned Brooks" as the author and that there are two books by Ned Brooks: *The Mythical Mammoth* and *No Free Lunch*.

DB: So, in this case, Ned enters the author and I will return a list with two books on it.

Search: So now I will *display list of Lendables*, in this case two Books, to the user. I will collaborate with User Interacter.

User Interacter: I will use my *display lendable list* responsibility. I will use a dialog box, which will contain the Lendable (using a *display lendable* responsibility I just added) and buttons that the user can push to navigate the list or end the search. In this scenario, Ed finishes perusing the two items on the list and then pushes "done."

Search: Then I give each Book (two in this case) back to DB.

DB: You know, I don't need to actually store the Book data in the database because nothing has changed. Perhaps I should have a separate *release* responsibility that just destroys the object.

Search: Okay, then, I release each Book (two in this case) with the help of DB and I am history, Librarian.

Librarian: Then Ned decides to "exit" the program (I get this from User Interacter as usual) and I *wait for user* yet again.

Jim says that although he understands what a Search needs to do at a high level, he will want to work closely with Cecilia during its implementation. She is more knowledgeable in both user interface and DBMS and will implement the DB and User Interacter class. Cecilia agrees that together they will work out the details of searching during implementation.

SCENARIOS, SCENARIOS, SCENARIOS

The group works through their entire list of scenarios, normal and exceptional, adding new ones as appropriate. Related scenarios, such as multiple transactions per session and checking out multiple lendables when the borrower is near their lendable limit, are also explored.

Exceptional scenarios, such as a borrower with overdue lendables checking out items, a borrower checking in overdue items, and a borrower searching for lendables that are not in the library can all be accommodated. New exceptional scenarios such as "What if the borrower is not in the database?" or "What if the database connection fails?" are handled as well. In order to handle exceptional behavior such as the last two scenarios, the team notes the use of the Error handling classes from the Tools.h++ library. The objects of this class that will be used in the system will be decided upon as implementation proceeds.

When to Start Prototyping

At some point in the design process, a group will decide that it is time to launch into code and begin to prototype the application. This will naturally be earlier in the process for experienced C++/O-O developers and later for teams just learning the new approach. Even for teams new to object-oriented design, there comes a point at which things are discussed and planned to such an extent that the detail begins to exceed English and "lapse" into code. The group members want to test their knowledge of the design in a prototype.

Chances are that group members have already done some prototyping of classes while design sessions have progressed. This can be productive and useful, as it helps to give team members a concrete feel for what the design is trying to accomplish. However, participants should resist the temptation to code in too much detail before class interfaces and interactions are fairly well specified. Doing so can lead to bias on the part of designers based on implementation strategy and usually results in rework of the code.

At some stage, the design has been specified well enough that members of the team go their separate ways and implement the classes for which they are responsible. Since every design decision will not be cast in stone before implementation begins, group reviews will resume whenever analysis and design questions come up in coding.

The Library application team members diverge as the designers move on to implementation. Jim and Cecilia each take the classes with which they have been working. That means that Jim has the Lendable hierarchy, Date, ID Verifier, Fine, and all Transactions. Cecilia takes Borrower, DB, and User Interacter. Since Cecilia is also responsible for database and user-interface modeling, Jim takes Betty's Librarian class as well. In Chapter 6, we discuss the issues they face and the decisions they make as they move the design to a C++ prototype. But before we delve into implementation, we will discuss the potential role of CRC card tools and ways to document a CRC card design.

Tools for CRC Card Design

In the past few years, a small set of tools have become available to support the use of CRC cards for analysis and design. The following discussion describes the purpose of these tools and how they can be used to support a project using CRC cards for their object-oriented development.

Why Use a Tool?

A CRC card tool should not be viewed as an attempt to automate the process we have described in Chapter 3 and continued in this chapter. As we mentioned in Chapter 2, an early attempt to create and use the cards in a software tool was abandoned by Ward Cunningham in favor of paper index cards. The success of the CRC card process lies in the human interaction fostered in the sessions that use them.

So why have a CRC card software tool at all? One reason is to provide a way to save the cards on-line as a permanent record of what is done in the sessions each day. While there is usually only one set of index cards, any number of sets can be generated by a tool to provide documentation to a wider audience. And some tools provide additional documentation, such as hierarchy graphs and collaboration graphs. Live prototypes are not always the best way to illustrate a CRC card model, especially to high-level management or even some customers. Tools can be used to demonstrate the system more formally and to a wider audience.

Some tools also provide a nice way of viewing the collaboration graph that is implicit in the cards. Analysis of this graph may lead to new design decisions to streamline collaborations or separate subsystems. A tool may also generate new cards to be used in further design sessions. This is useful if changes are made on-line or if many different designs have been tried and the cards have lines crossed out and overwritten. Some tools also have the ability to add implementation details such as class data members and to generate header file and member function stubs as the first step into prototyping.

What Is Available?

By far the most ambitious tool in the CRC card arena is **Object System/CRC™** from Rational. It runs under Windows and is the one fully supported and maintained product of which I am aware. There are CRC card tools that run under other platforms, such as the **CRC Card TOOL (CCOOL)** from AT&T Bell Laboratories for UNIX and Apple's **CRCCards** for the Macintosh. These are tools that, though developed for internal use, are now available to outside customers. The likelihood of additional upgrades to these tools is small, but they may be useful to support CRC card activities for customers on these platforms. The following provides a high-level description of each of the tools.

Object System/CRC

Object System/CRC supports the CRC card process at various levels. It can be used simply to record classes and their responsibilities, collaborators, and superclass/subclass relationships. This is done by entering text on a window that resembles an index card. This "card" can even be flipped so that comments and descriptions can be written on the back. The tool facilitates the process of filling in the card by providing drop-down lists of previously defined classes to use for collaborators, superclasses, and subclasses. Re-

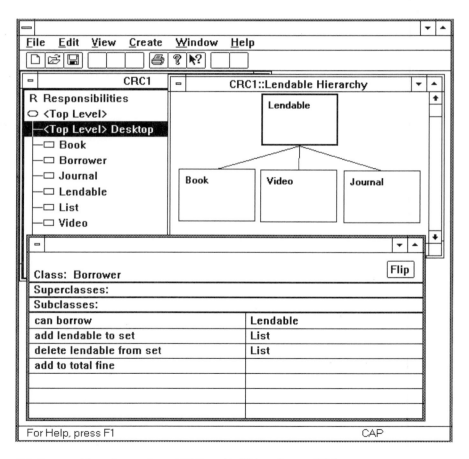

Figure 5.8 Browser, hierarchy graph, and CRC card in **Object System/CRC**.

sponsibilities can be detailed in a separate window where the set of operations that carries out this responsibility can be specified.

The classes can be viewed in various ways: as single cards, in a window showing all cards, or in a browser window, where the names of cards are listed, grouped by subsystem. The views are highly connected, and navigating among them is easy. New versions of the cards can be printed in various formats, including "real card" format of various sizes.

The tool also incorporates some of the notions of Wirfs-Brock's responsibility-driven design. If a user wants to group cards into named subsystems or responsibilities into contracts, the tool supports this. It will also create hierarchy graphs for any class. If the **Object System/CRC** user wants to use CRC card information as input to the Booch methodology, he or she can export the model from this tool to Rational Rose. Figure 5.8 shows the part of the **Object System/CRC** display for the Library application, including the Borrower CRC card and a hierarchy graph of the Lendable classes.

CCOOL

CCOOL has one main window for viewing the CRC card model, where the cards are created and displayed as icons. A card can be selected in the main window and the corresponding card window viewed on the screen for input or editing. There, the user inputs class names, super- and subclasses, attributes, responsibilities, and collaborators. Collaborations and superclass/subclass relationships can also be drawn as a link between two card icons in the main graphical display. The cards in hierarchies or subsystems can be stacked to unclutter the display.

CCOOL will generate header file and member function stubs from cards when the project is ready to begin prototyping. It has a reverse engineering capability as well; that is, it will read existing code and create cards, collaborations, and collaboration graphs as best as possible for the code. Figure 5.9 shows a **CCOOL** card and graphical display.

CRCCards

Apple's **CRCCards**, like **CCOOL**, has a main view with card icons. But this window does not contain any representation of relationships. It simply provides a way to keep track of which cards have been created. Selecting an icon causes the corresponding CRC card to appear. The user enters attributes, or fields, as well as responsibilities and

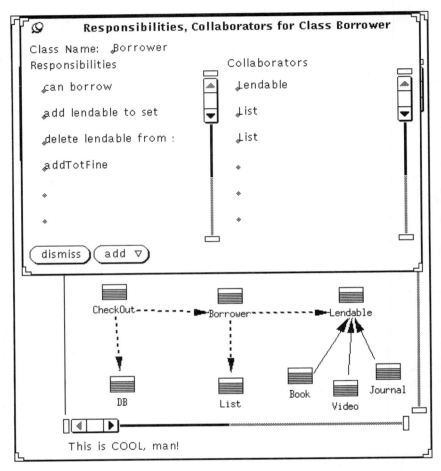

Figure 5.9 CCOOL display.

collaborators. This tool also allows the user to generate header files and stubs for member functions. It has options for which language to use and even lets the user choose what class library to assume. If the user chooses MacApp, for example, **CRC-Cards** will automatically edit names of fields and classes to follow the MacApp naming conventions. And it makes lists of the MacApp classes available from which to choose to serve as collaborators and superclasses. Figure 5.10 is a facsimile of the Borrower card in the **CRCCards** display.

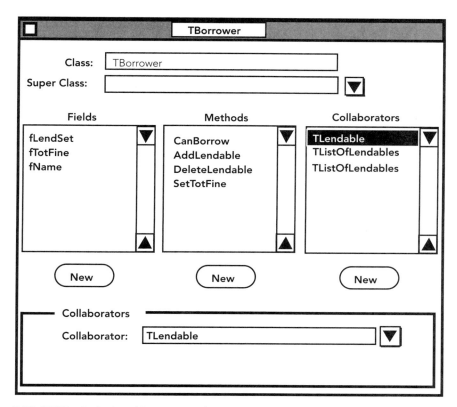

Figure 5.10 CRCCards display of Borrower card.

Documenting a CRC Card Design

Even for projects that do not use formal methods and notations, it is often necessary to convey the essence of a CRC card design in a written form. There is no prescribed notation for this documentation, but there are three types of information that together describe a CRC card design fairly completely: a class model, a set of class descriptions, and a set of scenario descriptions. Depending on a project's needs, different combinations of these may be generated. Exactly what written form this information takes depends upon the project. We will describe the types of information and give examples of realizations of these types for the Library application.

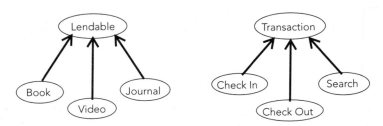

Figure 5.11 The Library application class model: hierarchies.

Class Model

The highest-level description of the design is one or more pictures showing classes and their relationships. This can be produced manually, as we have done in this book, or the graph may be produced by a CRC card tool. Superclass/subclass relationships can be shown on the same picture as collaborations or separately. Other tools may also be available to produce this picture, as many formal methodologists include such a graph as a part of their methods. As an example, let us look at the class model for the Library application. Figure 5.11 contains the class hierarchies for the application.

We have split the collaboration models for the Library application into three separate diagrams. Figures 5.12 and 5.13 contain collaborations for the interface classes, DB, and User Interacter, respectively. Figure 5.14 contains the collaboration model for the main application classes.

After the design sessions, the original problem model has been altered quite a bit. It has a slightly different set of classes and new responsibilities. Note that only the respon-

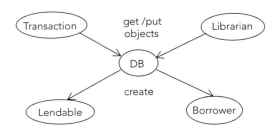

Figure 5.12 Library application class model: DB collaborations.

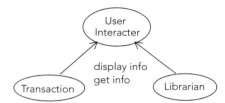

Figure 5.13 Library application class model: User Interacter collaborations.

sibilities needed by other classes are listed in this diagram. Responsibilities listed on the cards but not in this picture represent operations used only by the class itself.

Class Descriptions

If more detail about each class at a design level is desired, some sort of class description should be added. This may be as simple as a copy of the cards themselves. Some projects like to use a more comprehensive form of documentation where they can capture additional detail and more generous commenting. Use of a medium such as a UNIX manual page

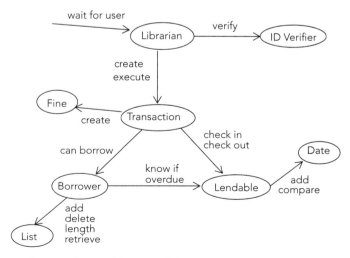

Figure 5.14 Library application class model: main collaborations.

allows a project to specify types of data passed and returned from responsibilities. Other projects use the header files, created manually or tool-generated. Man pages and header files are more appropriate after some prototyping has taken place. The class description should minimally contain high-level responsibilities for each class.

The following is a sample set of class descriptions for the Library application design. This information is transferred from the cards themselves, but the description and attributes are moved from the back of the card.

User Interacter:

Description: class that serves as interface to the User Interface subsystem

get employee ID	Views.h++ classes
get user action	Views.h++ classes
get lendable ID	Views.h++ classes
display message	Views.h++ classes
display ok or cancel message	Views.h++ classes
display lendable	Views.h++ classes
collect search info	Views.h++ classes
display lendable list	Views.h++ classes

Search:

Description: class whose objects execute searches and display lendables

execute	
get search criteria	User Interacter
get list of lendables	DB
display list	User Interacter

Borrower

Description: class whose objects represent employees who use the library

Attributes: name, total fine, set of lendables

create	List
can borrow	
know total fine amount	
know number of lendables	List
retrieve lendable from set	List
check overdue lendable	Lendable
add lendable to set	List
delete lendable from set	List

Table 5.1 Scenario 1: Check Out Checks Borrower Status.

Client	Server	Responsibility	Comment
Check Out	Borrower	can borrow	
Borrower	Borrower	know total fine	fine cannot be greater than $100
Borrower	List	number of entries	no more than 5 items out
Borrower	List	retrieve entry	for each lendable in set
Borrower	Lendable	know if overdue	ask if it is overdue
Lendable	Date	compare dates	compare due date with today

Scenario Descriptions

Since class models and class descriptions provide only static views of the application, they do not convey any sense of the flow of control of the system. The third type of information, scenario descriptions, describe how each scenario is fulfilled by the model. The addition of these to the set of documentation provides the necessary dynamic aspect.

The Jacobson notation[3] (as we saw in Chapter 4) is an excellent way to describe scenarios. A scenario table, such as the one used in Chapter 1, is not as effective but is easier to draw. Table 5.1 depicts of the fulfillment of a simple scenario.

In Chapter 3 (see Where Am I?), we briefly discussed relationships among scenarios. There was much repetition in the "end-to-end" scenarios that the Library team executed in Chapter 3 and in this chapter, and the group did not always feel the need to repeat portions that they had executed before in detail. We can view these repeated sections as small scenarios, since we consider a scenario to be any activity of the application that requires a collaboration. Therefore, most scenarios will actually be made up of many smaller scenarios.

For example, both check-out and return scenarios need a sequence of interactions that accomplish tasks such as obtaining a Lendable object (get the lendable ID via the User Interacter, get the Lendable object from the DB) and obtaining a Borrower object (get the employee ID via the User Interacter, get the Borrower object from the DB). Tables 5.2 and 5.3 describe these scenarios. Note that in these scenario tables, the initial client is referred to as *someone* because different types of objects will initiate this scenario at different times. By not specifying a particular initial client, the scenarios are more reusable. Also, notice that as we document scenarios, we group similar scenarios into more

Table 5.2 Scenario 2: Someone Gets a Lendable Object.

Client	Server	Responsibility	Comment
someone	DB	get Lendable	
DB	DB++ classes	get info from DBMS	get info from Lendable table
DB	Lendable	create	

general ones, e.g., check out a Lendable, rather than document each of the specific scenarios that drove the sessions separately, e.g., check out a Book, check out a Journal, and check out a Video.

There is a nesting relationship among scenarios that can be identified when executing them and utilized for a more efficient documentation. This can be seen in Table 5.3 where Scenario 3 uses Scenario 2 as a subset. The goal is to document scenarios in a modular manner, describing them in chunks that are large enough to be reused as a whole but small enough that pieces of them do not need to be repeated.

As a final example, consider the scenario, Check Out Checks Out Lendable, described in Table 5.4. Notice that some exceptional scenarios have been integrated with normal scenarios for documentation in this table. For example, if the user cannot borrow or if the lendable cannot be found or is already OUT, a message is displayed. A group may decide to document exceptional scenarios in separate tables. Such a group will want to make use of subscenarios, such as "Lendable checks itself out," to avoid repetition as much as possible.

Table 5.3 Scenario 3: Someone Gets a Borrower Object.

Client	Server	Responsibility	Comment
someone	DB	get Borrower	
DB	DB++ classes	get info from DBMS	get info from Borrower table
DB	Borrower	create	
Borrower	List	create	create empty set of lendables
DB	DB	Scenario 2	get lendables for Borrower's set
DB	Borrower	add lendable to set	add each lendable

Table 5.4 Scenario 3: Check Out Checks Out Lendable

Client	Server	Responsibility	Comment
Check Out	Borrower	Scenario 1	can borrow
Check Out	User Interacter	display message	if not, issue error message
Check Out	User Interacter	display message	if problem with lendable, issue error message
Check Out	Lendable	check out	
Lendable	Lendable	calculate due date	
Lendable	Date	add days to date	add days to today to determine due date
Lendable	Lendable	know due date	set due date information
Lendable	Lendable	know borrower	set borrower info to current borrower
Check Out	Borrower	add lendable to set	store the lendable

Summing Up

The goal of object-oriented design is to add details to the problem model that reflect decisions about the system's implementation. This may entail changing the model by adding or splitting classes to provide a better division of responsibilities. It certainly means adding classes and responsibilities to support system functions. Design decisions must be made in the context of design constraints such as target machine, environment, and language.

Detailing the design of an application in CRC card sessions provides continuity from problem modeling into design. The group setting sparks creative interactions and provides an excellent environment for learning how to make design decisions in an object-oriented context. The cards can be enhanced somewhat to capture more detailed design information. And a CRC card tool may be helpful for saving, illustrating, and documenting a design.

Coming Up

In the next chapter, we describe the process of moving a CRC card design to a C++ prototype. We discuss how CRC card design elements map to programming constructs, then describe sets of C++ features that can be used to implement design constructs. How to choose among the features and the implications of those choices in the implementation of an efficient C++ program are also explored.

References

1. Wirfs-Brock, Rebecca. "The Incremental Nature of Design." *SmallTalk Report* 2(1):10, 1993.
2. Booch, Grady. *Object-Oriented Analysis and Design with Applications,* 2nd ed. Benjamin-Cummings, Redwood City, CA, 1993.
3. Jacobson, Ivar, Magnus Christerson, Patrik Jonsson, and Gunnar Overgaard. *Object-Oriented Software Engineering.* Addison-Wesley, Reading, MA, 1992.

CHAPTER
6

Representing CRC Card Designs in C++

Programming a computer is still one of the most difficult tasks ever undertaken

by humankind; becoming proficient in programming requires talent, creativity,

intelligence, logic, the ability to build and use abstractions, and experience—

even when the best tools are available.

—Timothy Budd[1]

C++ WILL BE OUR LANGUAGE of choice for expressing a CRC card design in code. Moving this design to a C++ implementation is not a case of simple transliteration. It requires solid knowledge of the language and an understanding of how design constructs best map into language features. The purpose of this chapter is to help convey that understanding.

After a short history and discussion of C++, the chapter has two main parts. First we describe how CRC card components correspond to the syntax and features of C++. Then we illustrate how a C++ class is constructed from the information on the CRC card.

C++

C++[2] was invented by Bjärne Stroustrup at AT&T Bell Laboratories. It has been in use since 1980, when an early version of the language called "C with Classes" was developed and used by Stroustrup for major simulation projects. The name C++ was coined in 1983, the same year that the language was first available outside the group in which it was invented. C++ has its roots mostly in C[3], which remains as a subset, and Simula[4], which inspired the *class* feature. A C++ ANSI standardization effort was begun late in 1989 and is expected to be complete by the end of 1995.

Although its syntax overlaps with that of C, C++ adds direct language support for object-oriented design and programming concepts such as data abstraction, encapsulation and information hiding, superclass/subclass relationships, and polymorphism. C++ is now the dominant language for object-oriented technology in general, and almost absolutely so in the areas of systems programming and scientific applications.

The closeness of C++ to C is undeniably one reason for its enormous success and for the spread of object-oriented technology in general in recent years. C++ makes object-oriented programming accessible to the millions of programmers who already know C. However, learning C++ alone does not make one an object-oriented programmer. An understanding of the new paradigm at the analysis and design level is essential to writing an object-oriented program.

The first five chapters of this book have concentrated on the use of CRC cards to gain this understanding and to create an object-oriented model of an application. This chapter will describe how this model is best implemented in C++.

C++ Experience

In general, a developer moving a CRC card design to code should have some experience with C++. While it is true that learning C++ does not make you able to write object-oriented programs, it is just as true that learning about objects does not make you able to write good C++ programs. And the double learning curve of object design and C++ syntax and subtle semantics, if not planned for, can strangle a project.

A good approach is to learn the basics of C++ before, or perhaps in parallel with, learning about the object-oriented paradigm. Then, when it is time to implement the model, the basic concepts of the language are understood and are part of the developer's tool set. This initial knowledge of C++ should not be taken for granted. As Budd says, "Managers and programmers alike hope that a C [...] programmer can be changed into a C++ [...] programmer with no more effort than the addition of a couple of characters to the programmer's job description"[1]. In reality, this is a nontrivial step in the process.

Basic C++ knowledge by the developer is assumed in the implementation described here. The reader who needs to refresh his or her knowledge of C++ syntax and features is referred to books by Lippman[5] and Stroustrup[6]. In this chapter, we describe how elements of a CRC card design map to these features. Also, we try to convey how basic C++ knowledge is effectively applied to the development of classes when moving from an object-oriented design to code. The reader is referred to books by Murray[7] and Meyers[8] for more in-depth discussions of the effective and efficient use of C++.

C++ Naming Conventions

We will adopt certain naming conventions for our C++ code examples. We will follow the common convention that a C++ class name begins with an uppercase letter. Function names and identifier names in our examples will begin with a lowercase letter. Exceptions to this rule are constructors, which, because they share the name of the class, begin with an uppercase letter, e.g., Librarian(), and the destructor, which begins with a "~", e.g., ~Librarian().

Names in C++ must be a single word. Multiple-word CRC card class, responsibility, and attribute names generally translate to a single C++ name in one of two ways. The first word always follows the convention for the type of name. Subsequent words are either capitalized and then concatenated, e.g., IdVerifier and waitForUser(), or not capitalized and connected to previous words by an underscore, e.g., Id_verifier and wait_for_user(). We prefer the former method, and examples in this chapter will follow this style. Neither method is intrinsically better than the other. Consistency is the most important thing.

CRC to C++

Developing an object-oriented C++ application means defining a set of C++ classes using design data as input. Each C++ class will contain:

♦ Data members that represent the design class state and form the physical representation of the class

♦ Member function declarations (with appropriate signatures and specifiers) that declare the behavior of the objects of that class, including:
  – C++ class-specific functions that specify how objects are created and destroyed
  – functions that reflect application behavior

♦ Member function implementations that define the behavior of the class

Defining these classes requires that we know how design information contributes to the definition of the class. The next section describes how the CRC design elements map to C++ features. Once we are familiar with these mappings, we can begin to build the classes, making choices when necessary among C++ features and applying effective C++ coding practices in their implementation.

CRC Elements as C++ Constructs

Each of the elements of a CRC card design (class, responsibility, collaborator, attribute, superclass, subclass) correspond to a particular language construct, or set of constructs, which can be used to represent them.

Class

In design, classes represent the important entities in the problem and solution domains. As such, they form the framework for the design model. When moving from design to C++, CRC classes provide input to the formation of a set of C++ classes, which will form a framework for the implementation. Each CRC design class will map to a C++ class; that is, for each CRC card, we will create a class in C++. In upcoming sections, we describe how the CRC card design elements on a single card will help to define the C++ class corresponding to that card.

C++ class names are simply the CRC card class name altered to follow our conventions. The following is the first step toward the C++ class declaration corresponding to the Borrower class in the Library design:

```
class Borrower {
   // class definition
};
```

Implementing a CRC card class may actually result in more than one C++ class. Additional classes may be created during development to carry out the implementation of the design classes, or classes may be added to the code for testing and debugging during development. Finally, the introduction of error-handling classes to deal with exceptional situations often takes place during this development phase.

Responsibility

In design, the responsibilities of a class define the knowledge it maintains and the services that it offers. When moving from design to C++, CRC card responsibilities provide input to the object's internal representation and help to define a set of C++ member functions for the class.

Since *know* responsibilities reflect a design object's state, they will provide clues (along with attributes and other collaborations) for determining the data members that make up its physical representation. For example, the fact that Borrower has a responsibility to *know total fine* is a strong clue that a data member to represent the total fine, e.g., totalFine, will be needed.

The most important contribution of the responsibilities, however, will be as a framework for the set of member functions of the class. Some responsibilities will correspond directly to one member function. For example, a responsibility called *create* will likely correspond to a C++ constructor. Another example of this one-to-one mapping is Borrower's *can borrow* responsibility, which will be implemented as a member function with the name canBorrow().

Sometimes a responsibility written on a CRC card is at a higher level than a single member function. At development time, it must be further decomposed into the appropriate set of functions. For example, *know* responsibilities that still appear on cards often represent a pair of C++ functions to retrieve and update state information. The Entry class in the Checkbook example, for instance, has a *know amount* responsibility. When implementing a Checkbook program, this responsibility could spur the creation of two member functions to retrieve and update this information, perhaps called howMuch() and setAmount().

Sometimes a responsibility is at a lower level than an entire member function; that is, it may correspond to a single message that needs to be sent to a collaborator. In C++, this type of responsibility will be implemented as a line inside a member function. Many of our subresponsibilities fall into this category. For example, Check Out has a subresponsibility to *check the borrower's status* as part of its *create* responsibility. During implementation, this will correspond to a single line within CheckOut's constructor, as follows:

```
// constructor
CheckOut::CheckOut(Borrower* bp, const String& lendID)
{
   if (bp->canBorrow() == FALSE) {    // here it is
      //...
   }
   //...
}
```

On the other hand, more design may need to take place at this stage to clarify how a CRC card responsibility corresponds to member functions. For example, DB's *get information from dbms* may represent a set of messages sent within a single function or a set of messages across a set of functions. An important part of the job of moving a CRC card design to a C++ program is noting what each responsibility means in terms of member functions.

Collaborator

In design, we list a collaborator next to a responsibility when the fulfillment of the responsibility requires sending a message to an object of the collaborator's type. When moving from design to C++, collaborations provide input to the signatures and implementation of the initiator's member functions, as well as to its physical representation.

A number of different design relationships may exist between collaborating class objects. If A and B are CRC card design classes, the types of collaboration relationships that can exist between them are the following:

- ◆ class A **uses-a** object of class B

- ◆ class A **has-a** object of class B

- ◆ class A **has-a** class B

Each of these is represented in a different way in a C++ program and provides inputs to different parts of a C++ class. So the best way to describe the mapping of collaborations to C++ constructs is to explore in more detail each of these design relationships.

USES-A RELATIONSHIP

The most general collaboration relationship that exists between an initiator class and its collaborating class is the class-to-object **uses-a** relationship. Indeed, every collaboration in our model represents an instance of this relationship. This simply implies that a class needs a responsibility of (or sends a message to) an object of the collaborator class. For instance, a Checkbook object **uses-a** Check object when it sends it a *generate* message, and a Game object **uses-a** Pitcher object when it sends it the *pitch* message.

In C++, if A and B are classes and A **uses-a** B object, it means that a member function of B is called on a B object within a member function of A. In C++, the **.** operator is used to send a message to, or call a member function of, an object. The -> operator is used when a pointer to an object receives the message. For example, when Checkbook collaborates with Check, it means that a member function of Check is called on a Check object within a member function of Checkbook as follows:

```
Checkbook::printCheck(const Check& check)
{
  // p is a Printer
  check.generate(p);    // Check collaboration
}
```

Similarly, Game collaborates with Pitcher by sending the pitch() message to a Pitcher object within a Game member function:

```
Game::begin()
{
  // thePitcher is a Pitcher*
  thePitcher->pitch();    // Pitcher collaboration
}
```

In the Library application design, we see on the Librarian CRC card (Figure 6.1) that this class has a responsibility to *get and verify employee ID* as a subresponsibility of *wait*

Librarian	
wait for user	
get and verify employee ID	User Interacter
	ID Verifier
know current borrower	DB
initiate transaction	User Interacter
	Transaction
display error message	User Interacter

Figure 6.1 Librarian CRC card.

for user. We also see that it needs to collaborate with User Interacter and ID Verifier in order to fulfill this responsibility. This could be represented in a C++ member function as follows:

```
void
Librarian::waitForUser()
{
   // user is the User Interacter object
   IdVerifier idVer;
   String empID;
   while((empID=user.getEmployeeId()) != "goodnight") {
     if (idVer.verify() == 0) {
       user.displayMessage("Invalid user");
       continue;
     }
     // ...
   }
}
```

We say that Librarian **uses-a** UserInteracter and IdVerifier because it calls member functions of these classes to complete its task. It sends getEmployeeId() and display-Message() messages to user, the UserInteracter object, and a verify() message to idVer, the IdVerifier object.

Thus, **uses-a** collaborations provide input to the implementation of member functions because they imply what messages need to be sent to implement an operation. We can gain even more information from this collaboration by knowing the form of the collaborating object. The collaborator could be known to all objects, such as an object of an interface class, e.g., user. Or it could be local to the member function because its lifetime is the same as the invocation of a single function. The idVer object is an example of this type of collaborator.

Often it is the case that the collaborator object has been passed to the initiator's member function. An example of this is the Checkbook collaboration we saw earlier. When this is the case, the collaboration provides additional information about the argument types of the initiator's member function. Finally, the collaborator could be a data member of the initiating class. This is the relationship we will explore next.

CLASS-TO-OBJECT **HAS-A** RELATIONSHIP

The second kind of relationship that may exist between collaborating classes is the class-to-object **has-a** relationship. This relationship exists when an object of the collaborator class is conceptually part of the state of the initiator class. This is evident most often in collaborations for *know* responsibilities, but any collaboration could imply that the collaborator object is in the state of the class. For example, the Game class **has-a** Pitcher object and the Check Out class **has-a** Borrower object.

In C++, if A and B are classes and A **has-a** B object, it means that an object of type B is in A's physical representation; that is, an object (or a pointer or a reference to an object) of type B is an actual data member of A.

The simplest way to represent the **has-a** relationship in C++ is to use an actual object as a member of the class. For example, the Lendable class has a responsibility to *know due date* with Date listed as the collaborator. This implies that Lendable has-a Date object in its state, which it maintains. In C++, this could be implemented as follows:

```
class Lendable {
  // ...
  Date dueDate;
};
```

But the relationship may also be implemented with a member of pointer or reference type. For instance, the Borrower member of the CheckIn class will be represented with a pointer member as follows:

```
class CheckIn {
  // ...
  Borrower* currBorr;
};
```

Once it is known that a class-to-object **has-a** relationship exists, the developer of the C++ class must decide whether the class should contain an actual object or a pointer or reference to an object. This decision will be based on the design model being implemented as well as efficiency considerations. See the Choosing C++ Data Members section later in this chapter for a detailed discussion of the trade-offs of this decision when building classes.

CLASS-TO-CLASS **HAS-A** RELATIONSHIP

A class-to-class **has-a** relationship exists when one class only has meaning in the context of another class. This can be reflected in any collaboration but is often associated with the collaborator in a *know* responsibility. A common example is a Link class that is used to represent the nodes and links in a linked list. It is used only by the List class, and no other class needs to know it even exists.

In C++, if A and B are classes and A **has-a** B class, it means that class B's declaration is within the scope of A's declaration. It also implies that only A can directly manipulate objects of class B. A class defined within another class in C++ is referred to as a *nested class*. A class-to-class has-a relationship usually implies that a class-to-object **has-a** relationship exists as well. That is, an object (or pointer or reference to an object) of the nested class is most likely also a member of the enclosing class.

In the case of the List class mentioned above, Link should be a nested class of List, and a pointer to a Link object is also a member of the class.

```
class List {
// ...
private:
  class Link { ... };
  Link* head;// a member as well
};
```

To find candidates for class-to-class **has-a** relationships and nested classes in the implementation, we look at classes that are only used by one other class in the design. For instance, the Date class is only used by classes in the Lendable hierarchy. It could be implemented as a nested class. As it turns out, Jim will not implement it this way because he decides to reuse the RogueWave general purpose Date[1] class to represent these objects.

---

[1]All class names in the Rogue Wave library are actually prefixed with RW to avoid name clashes with other libraries and user's own classes. For simplicity, in this chapter we will refer to Rogue Wave classes without the prefix.

Another potential candidate for a nested class is the ID Verifier class, which is only used by the Librarian class. In a previous example, an object of this class was local to Librarian's waitForUser() member function, but why not make it an object of a nested class of Librarian as follows?

```
class Librarian {
  // ...
  class IdVerifier {
    // implementation
  };
  IdVerifier idVer; // a member as well
};
```

Classes added for the implementation of another class are also often declared to be nested classes.

Strictly speaking, a class-to-class **has-a** relationship does not have to be implemented as a nested class in C++, but it should be. In C++, all nonnested class names reside in the global namespace. As the number of class names grows, the likelihood of name clashes increases, especially when reusing third-party software. When possible, nested classes should be used to avoid cluttering the global namespace.

Attributes

In design, attributes listed on the back of the CRC card help describe the logical state of a design object. They are the characteristics of a class or the knowledge that the class maintains to support the services it provides to other classes of objects.

When moving from design to C++, attributes provide input to the physical representation of a class as well as some member functions of the class. The element of the state represented by an attribute may be stored in the class as a member object (or pointer or reference to an object). These data members may be elements used only by objects of the class, or they may be requested or changed by other objects and so imply the existence of functions that retrieve or modify the information. In many situations, attribute information overlaps input from *know* responsibilities.

For example, the attributes that Betty suggested and Jim listed for the Fine class were lendable, borrower, fine amount, due date, and returned date. These could be implemented by Jim as actual data members of C++ class Fine as follows:

```
class Fine {
  Lendable* lend;
  Borrower* borr;
  double amount;
  Date dueDate;
  Date returnedDate;
  // ...
};
```

As we add to the set of data members of a class from the design attributes, we will again need to make decisions about what types of variables will be used in the class, just as with class-to-object **has-a** relationships discovered through collaborations, e.g., how did we decide that a Lendable* should be a member of Fine? And why not use a Lendable object? For some insights on this decision as we build C++ classes, see the section Choosing C++ Data Members.

Superclass/Subclass Relationships

In design, the existence of superclasses and subclasses implies an **is-a** relationship between design classes. A subclass **is-a** kind of its superclass, and it will share, and perhaps expand upon, the superclass state and behavior.

When moving from design to C++, this relationship is implemented in one of two ways. The most common implementation of a superclass/subclass relationship is with public inheritance. Superclasses become *base classes* in C++. They will implement the most generic behavior for classes in their hierarchy. Subclasses become *publicly derived classes*. They will automatically inherit the data members and member functions of their base classes. They will probably add some data and operations and may redefine some of the base class behavior.

For example, the Lendable and Transaction hierarchies in the Library application will be implemented with public inheritance, as would the following Entry hierarchy from the Checkbook example.

```
class Entry {
  // Entry-specific stuff
};

class WithdrawalEntry : public Entry {
  // Withdrawal-specific stuff
};
```

```
class DepositEntry : public Entry {
  // Deposit-specific stuff
};

class CheckEntry : public WithdrawalEntry {
  // Check-specific stuff
};
```

Note that when declaring a C++ class, the names of the base classes are listed on the declaration line with the public specifier.

Certain responsibilities on a superclass card are repeated on the cards of each subclass, e.g., *calculate fine* in the Lendable hierarchy and *execute* in the Transaction classes. This implies that these responsibilities are carried out differently by the subclasses in a way appropriate to them. A member function that corresponds to this type of responsibility is declared to be *virtual* in the base class.

A base class in C++ may be an *abstract base class* or a *concrete base class.* These features of C++ correspond to the notions of abstract and concrete superclasses described in Chapter 1 (see the section on Superclass/Subclass Relationships). The programmer declares a base class to be abstract by declaring at least one of its member functions to be a *pure virtual function.* This type of function is described later, but here is an example for the Lendable class:

```
class Lendable {
  // ...
  virtual double calculateFine() = 0;
};
```

The effect of declaring a base class to be abstract is that attempting to create an object of that type will be flagged as an error by the compiler. The Lendable class will be declared abstract because, although Lendable holds the data and operations common to all classes derived from Lendable (Book, Video, and Journal), no objects of type Lendable should actually exist in a program.

It is also possible that the best way to implement a set of classes in a hierarchy is not with inheritance at all, but with a single parameterized class. For example, a design might contain a class, List, that defines generic behavior, such as adding and deleting items. There may also be subclasses of List, such as List of integer, List of string, or List of lendables, which redefine this behavior in a way appropriate to the type that the List contains. In actuality, this behavior is the "same" across subclasses and does not depend at all on the type of object being held. The algorithms that describe the behavior can be *parameterized* by this type. Therefore, in the C++ implementation, List should be described as a single parameterized class, i.e., List<T> as follows:

```
template <class T>
class List {
public:
   void addItem(T);
   T deleteItem(T);
   // ...
private:
   class Link<T> {
     T* data;
     Link<T>* next;
   };
   Link<T>* head;
};
```

As Meyers[8] sums it up, templates should be used when the type of the object does not affect the implementation of the functions of the classes. Inheritance should be used when the type of the object does affect the implementation of the functions.

CRC Card Enhancements

In Chapter 5, we described how CRC cards may be enhanced to capture more detailed information during CRC card design sessions. We already discussed how subresponsibilities can provide input to member function implementation. The other two enhancements are the collaborating responsibility and the data that is passed with a collaboration.

When moving from design to C++, the collaborating responsibility will be the name of the message sent to the collaborating object. Thus, it provides input to both the implementation of the member function of the class that initiates the collaboration (by indicating which collaborator function should be called) as well as to the public interface of the collaborator class.

The data passed with the collaboration to help that object carry out its appointed task will be represented as the set of arguments to the collaborator's member function. Thus, it provides direct input to the types of arguments. This information will also help in the implementation of the member function of the initiating class by indicating what arguments should be passed to the collaborating function.

Scenarios

In design, scenarios are used to drive the discovery of classes and the distribution of responsibilities and attributes to those classes. The object-oriented model that emerges from a session can be exercised to show how the chosen set of classes, responsibilities, and collaborators fulfills each scenario. An important part of the documentation of a design is the set of descriptions detailing these interactions.

When moving from design to code, these scenarios will be a reminders to the implementer of what the finished application is trying to accomplish. Developers can use documentation such as the Jacobson[9] use case diagrams or the scenario tables we built in Chapter 5 to help remind them what needs to happen at each point. But most of the power of scenarios as input to implementation will be the knowledge of the design gained by the participants in the sessions.

Scenarios will also form the basis for a set of unit and system tests. As developers refer to scenarios to implement each function, they can use them to organize their unit tests as well. And system testers can use the scenario list as a basis for their test suite. The testers will be most effective if they have participated in analysis and design sessions or have attended special sessions where the problem model or design was demonstrated for them. As in the implementation phase, the documentation can help organize and complete the test cases, but most important will be the strong sense of the system gained by the execution of scenarios in the sessions.

Building C++ Classes from CRC Cards

Now that we understand how the elements of our CRC card design can be represented in C++, we can build prototype C++ classes drawing from these design elements as appropriate. The process of defining a C++ class from a CRC card class entails:

◆ Choosing and defining C++ data members that represent the class state from the CRC card attributes, *know* responsibilities, and collaborations

◆ Choosing C++ member functions that encompass CRC card class responsibilities

♦ Declaring the member functions within the class with return types and signatures that reflect CRC card collaborations

♦ Adding the appropriate function specifiers (inline, const, and virtual) with input from CRC card responsibilities, collaborations, and scenarios

♦ Implementing the member functions with input from CRC card subresponsibilities, collaborations, and scenarios

This list is not meant to imply a strict order; this is an extremely iterative process. For example, we usually develop an initial set of data members, then modify them as we know more about member functions and what is needed to support their implementation. In particular, the sense of what needs to happen in the application gained in the CRC card sessions, though formally set down in the implementation step, pervades each step described. We will present the steps in order here simply for illustrative purposes.

As we build the classes, we will concentrate on the Borrower and Lendable classes as examples. This will illustrate how issues apply to both a base class and a nonbase C++ class.

The following sections will describe what the developer will place inside the class definition. For a discussion of the most common view of a C++ application from the outside, see the section C++ File Organization later in the chapter.

Choosing C++ Data Members

The data members of the C++ class will be the set of variables that describe the state of the class and implement its physical representation. The initial set of data members usually corresponds closely to the design state of the class, and others are added later to support the operations or implementations of responsibilities. To implement this initial set of data members, we look at any attributes that have been listed. We also look at *know* responsibilities and collaborations and decide whether the collaborating object should actually be a member of the class.

As we declare C++ variables to represent class data members, we decide what C++ types best describe them. In order to do that, we need to understand the implications and trade-offs of using objects and pointers and references to objects as C++ data members.

DATA MEMBERS IN C++: POINTER, REFERENCE, OR OBJECT?

Once we know that a C++ class, say Thing, should have a member of class Mem, how do we decide if that member is a Mem object, a Mem*, or a Mem&? This choice is almost never arbitrary. In many cases, the design model of the class points to the use of a particular form for the member. Even in cases in which the developer has a choice, issues and trade-offs in terms of efficiency and simplicity can be delineated to aid in the decision. The following is a discussion of these issues.

If the data member refers to an object that already exists outside the scope of the class, then either a pointer data member or a reference member must be used. A reference member implies a particular set of design intentions. A reference to a Mem object should only be used as a member of class Thing when (1) the data member refers to an existing Mem object, (2) a Thing object does not make sense if that Mem member is not initialized (that is, a null value for the member has no meaning in the context of class Thing), and (3) that member refers to the same Mem object for the lifetime of the Thing object.[2]

Classes that represent relationships can often take advantage of reference members. For instance, a Call class (an association of two Telephone objects) fits this design model. A Call object exists simply to associate two existing Telephone objects; thus, it makes no sense for one of its Telephone members to be null. And neither Telephone member can refer to a different Telephone object for the lifetime of the Call (disregarding the notion of forwarding a call). So one way to implement the Call class in C++ would be as follows:

```
class Call {
public:
  // ...
private:
  Telephone& caller;  // bound once to existing
  Telephone& callee;  // Telephone objects
};
```

The reference members will require a particular type of initialization in the Call constructor. We will see an example of this later.

This is the only situation in which a reference member makes sense. In contrast, a pointer member should be used to point to an existing object whenever it makes sense for the member to have a null value at some point, and/or it can refer to different objects during the lifetime of the enclosing object.

---

[2]Recall that in C++, a variable of reference type is initialized as it is created and can never be changed to refer to an object other than that with which it was initialized. Indeed, every use of a reference after its initialization is actually a use of the object it refers to.

It is most often the case that the data member does not refer to an existing object; that is, the enclosed object is created by, and is only accessible to, the enclosing class. In these cases, the most straightforward way to implement the member is as an actual object of a class. The advantage of a member object is its simplicity and the fact that the memory management is handled automatically. For example, if class Book has a Date object member, as shown here, the Date object will be created on the stack each time a Book object is created.

```
class Book : public Lendable {
private:
  Date pubDate;
  //...
};
```

One disadvantage of a member object is that its size, if it is large or has the potential to be large, will have a negative impact on the size of the enclosing object. This can be a concern if collections of objects of the enclosing class will be created or if numerous copies of the enclosing object will be performed.

For example, String classes are usually defined as a pointer to another class that holds its representation, e.g.,

```
class String {
public:
  // ...
private:
  struct StringRep {
    StringRep(char*,int);
    ~StringRep();
    char* str;
    int len;
  };
  StringRep* srep;
};
```

This technique ensures that the size of String is small (1 byte) and consistent; that is, the size of the String per se will be independent of the number of characters it holds.

Using a pointer member, however, requires that we take on the responsibility of managing the memory associated with the member object. We need to dynamically allocate memory for the object on the heap whenever an object of the enclosing class is created (probably in the constructor) and remember to deallocate it when the object is destroyed (probably in the destructor). The following shows one constructor and the destructor for the String class discussed above.

```
String::String(char* s) : srep(new StringRep(s, strlen(s)))
{ }

String::~String() { delete srep; }
```

An object member only makes sense when the lifetime of the state element is the same as the lifetime of the object that contains it. Its value can change, but the object cannot be reincarnated. For example, the Date object, dueDate, in Lendable can change value, but the object itself lives and dies with the Lendable object. If we need a member that can hold different objects within the lifetime of the enclosed object, then a pointer member is appropriate.

An example from the Library application is Librarian's current borrower member, currBorr. This member is null when the Librarian object is first created and between sessions. The currBorr member is only set when an employee logs in and will refer to different Borrowers throughout the lifetime of the Librarian. Therefore, a Borrower* is appropriate for the type of this member.

Whether the member refers to an existing object or is created by the enclosing class, a pointer (or reference, when the earlier conditions hold) to an object *must* be used whenever the value assigned to the data member will actually be an object of a derived class. This is because only a pointer (or reference) to a base class can hold the address of (or refer to) a derived class object.

For example, a Chess program might define the class ChessBoard to be a collection of ChessSquare objects, each of which has a ChessPiece member as an occupant. The ChessPiece member will actually be declared as a pointer member, as follows.

```
class ChessSquare {
public:
// ...

private:
  ChessPiece* occupant;
  // ...
};
```

The first reason for such a declaration is that the contents of the occupant member will change over the lifetime of a ChessSquare object. A more important consideration, however, is that the member will actually point to an object of a class derived from ChessPiece, e.g., Pawn, Queen, or Bishop. We will see another example of this in the next section when Cecilia begins to implement the Borrower class.

A pointer member is sometimes used to implement a one-to-many class-to-object **has-a** relationship. For example, an IntArray class will actually have numerous integers as members, but it might be implemented with a single pointer member as follows:

```
class IntArray {
  //...
  int* array;
  int length;
};
```

The array member will be allocated space for many integers in the IntArray constructor. It is often the case that a one-to-many **has-a** relationship is implemented with a member whose type is a collection class of some sort, e.g., List, Set, or Array. In either case, the type of the elements of the array or the collection class are subject to the issues we have discussed in this section and need to be chosen carefully.

Next we will take a look at how Library application developers determine the physical representation for two of the Library classes. In this section we will use the information on the cards to determine the initial set of data members used to represent the C++ class. As development proceeds, other data members needed to support them will undoubtedly be added.

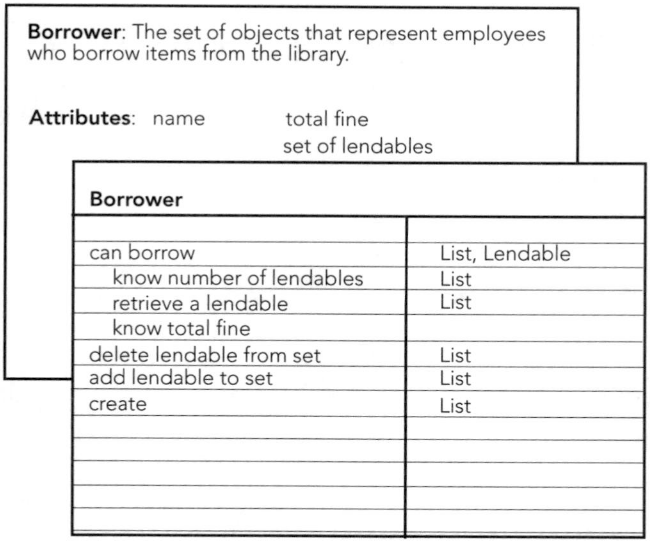

Borrower: The set of objects that represent employees who borrow items from the library.

Attributes: name total fine set of lendables

Borrower	
can borrow	List, Lendable
know number of lendables	List
retrieve a lendable	List
know total fine	
delete lendable from set	List
add lendable to set	List
create	List

Figure 6.2 Borrower CRC card.

BORROWER

As Cecilia considers what data members should be part of the Borrower class, she will examine the attributes, responsibilities, and collaborations on the Borrower CRC card. Figure 6.2 shows the Borrower card Cecilia took away from the design sessions. She first scans the collaborators to look for candidates for types of data members. Cecilia can see by looking at this card that Borrower collaborates with two other classes: List and Lendable. So objects of the C++ class implementations of these design classes are candidates for Borrower data members. Other members of user-defined types may also exist. Responsibilities with no collaborators sometimes signal members that are objects of a built-in type.

Next, Cecilia examines the list of attributes on the back of the card. The possibility of a member of List type is strengthened by the existence of the attribute, set of lendables, which she decided in design sessions should be implemented by a general purpose List class. Now Cecilia needs to decide what the exact type of this List member should be. She takes a closer look at the Rogue Wave library documentation and the responsibilities she needs the List to help fulfill.

The operations that Borrower will require from its List collaborator are knowing the number of elements, adding elements, deleting elements, and retrieving elements. The set will be small, so Cecilia decides that she does not need to choose a doubly linked list for efficiency. Therefore, she selects a singly linked list for simplicity. The library contains two types of singly linked list classes: one that hold objects (TValSlist<T>) and one that holds pointers to objects (TPtrSlist<T>).

In design, the team talked about the List holding Lendables. The collaboration with the List elements was said to be with Lendable, but it was actually collaborating with one of Lendable's subclasses. Cecilia realizes that in the code, there will be no Lendable objects, only objects of the derived classes. If she wants the List to be able to hold Book, Video, and Journal objects simultaneously, she must declare it to hold pointers to Lendable.[3] So she chooses the Rogue Wave TPtrSlist<T> class as the type for the data member, lendSet.

The last collaborator for Borrower is Lendable. Does this imply a separate Lendable member? Cecilia knows from the design sessions that the Borrower collaborates with Lendable via its *know if overdue* responsibility. She needs to ask this question of each of her previously borrowed items is overdue. But these are just the items that are in the List

---

[3]Remember that variables of type Base* can actually point to objects of any class derived from Base.

that she has already declared as a member. Borrower will collaborate with each Book, Video, or Journal as it is retrieved from the List. So there is no separately declared Lendable member.

Cecilia looks over the rest of the responsibilities and attributes. Most of the responsibilities exist to maintain the set of lendables. The remaining responsibility is *know total fine*, and a *know* responsibility often signals a member. This possibility is solidified by the presence of a total fine attribute on the back of the card. Since there is no collaboration for the *know total fine* responsibility, Cecilia first considers a built-in double type to represent her fine member. But then she remembers that in her study of the libraries she noticed a Money class that had some advantages over built-in types for handing decimal fractions. She decides to use an object of this type to represent totalFine.

The only piece of information on the Borrower card unaccounted for at this point is the name attribute. Cecilia decides to use the general purpose String class to represent this data member.

Both the name and totalFine members should have the same lifetime as a Borrower object, and the size of Borrower should not be an issue. Therefore, Cecilia decides to use actual objects of type Money and String to represent them. Thus, her first implementation of the physical representation for class Borrower looks like the following:

```
class Borrower {
public:
// ...

private:
   String name;
   Money totalFine;
   TPtrSlist<Lendable> lendSet;
};
```

LENDABLE

Figure 6.3 contains the CRC card for Jim's Lendable class from the Library application design. Jim will concentrate on the attributes, *know* responsibilities, and collaborators in his search for candidates for data members. Since Date is a collaborator for many responsibilities, it is an obvious type to consider for a member, or members, of Lendable. The attribute list also mentions a due date, and the front of the card lists a responsibility to *know due date*. So Jim first implements one Date member called dueDate.

Jim next looks at the *know if overdue* responsibility. Should there be a data member to represent this knowledge? Jim remembers that he and Cecilia decided during a design session that this information should be calculated each time it is needed. There will be a member function corresponding to this responsibility, but no data member.

The rest of the *know* responsibilities match attributes listed on the Lendable card. For example, there is a borrower attribute and a responsibility to *know borrower*. Does this imply that there is a member of type Borrower? Well, Borrower does not appear on the collaboration list, so we know Lendable never needs to send a message to it. Why does it need to know the borrower at all? Jim decides to have a design consultation with Cecilia about this.

Cecilia reminds Jim that the Check In class needs to ask DB for a new Borrower based on a lendable ID if the person returning the book is different from the original borrower. This implies that the Lendable database table has Borrower information. Therefore, the Lendable class must store that information when a Book, Video, or Journal is checked out. Jim agrees but claims that he does not need an actual Borrower object as part of Lendable, just some indication of who the borrower is. What should he use? Cecilia wonders if the name will do, but Jim quickly points out that employee names are not unique. Eventually, they realize they need a way to uniquely identify a Borrower, and

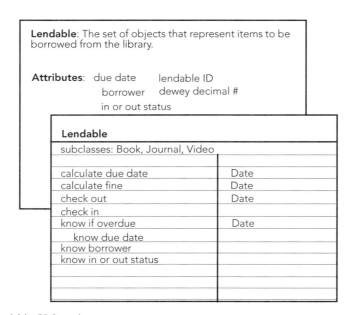

Figure 6.3 Lendable CRC card.

they settle upon the employee ID for this purpose. Jim decides that he will use this ID to indicate the borrower in his Lendable class with String borrowerID. Cecilia thinks that is a good idea and adds a borrower ID (String borrowerID) to her recently finished representation of the Borrower class.

The last *know* responsibility on the Lendable card is *know in or out status.* As Jim thinks about the in or out status, he realizes that Lendable's knowledge of a due date and borrower only make sense for a lendable that is "out." This implies that these data members need to have a null value when the Lendable is "in," and he wonders what value he should choose to represent a null Date object. More troubling to Jim is that Lendable has attributes that may be meaningless for some objects of the class. He is just beginning to think they should reconvene design sessions to deal with this when he has an inspiration.

His idea is to create a class to hold the "out" information (dueDate and borrowerID) and declare a pointer to that class to be a member of Lendable. The pointer has value 0 if the Lendable is "in"; otherwise, it points to an object of the OutRecord class. Thus, checking out the Lendable means creating an instance of this class. No other class need know this class exists, so Jim defines OutRecord as a nested class of Lendable. He wonders if he should discuss this decision with the design team but decides that is unnecessary as long as he sticks to the interface they decided upon.

The last two attributes from the Lendable CRC card are the dewey decimal number and the lendable ID. Since both of these are alphanumeric, they will be represented in Lendable as String members, deweyDecimalNumber and lendableID.

Finally, Jim looks at the rest of the responsibilities that collaborate with Date to determine if they collaborate with the same Date object or whether he might have to consider adding another Date member. The *calculate fine* and *calculate due date* responsibilities certainly will use the dueDate member of the OutRecord class. Both of these responsibilities will also need the object that represents the current date, today. In the design sessions, the team gave Date the responsibility to *know today's date.* But does the general purpose Date class fulfill this responsibility?

Some investigation into the library reveals that the Date class can be used to create a today object by initializing a Date object with 0. But Jim decides that it will be too expensive to create this object each time this information is requested. The today object should be created once and stored somewhere. Jim shifts the *know today's date* responsibility to Lendable and lists Date as a collaborator. He implements today as a static member of the Lendable C++ class. He could make it global variable; but why clog the global namespace[4] when Lendable is the only one who uses the variable? Later he will add a static member function to retrieve this information.

Thus far, the set of Lendable data members are the following:

```
class Lendable {
// ...
private:
  static Date today;

  String lendableID;
  String deweyDecimalNumber;
  class OutRecord {
    Date dueDate;
    String borrowerID;
  };
  OutRecord* out;
};
```

DATA MEMBERS AS PRIVATE MEMBERS

Once the C++ variables to represent the state of a class are chosen, they should be declared as private data members[5] of the class. Keeping data members private ensures that programs cannot change members in a way that is inconsistent with the proper use of the class. Also, representing the state with private members allows the class author to change the underlying representation of the class without breaking existing code. Keeping data private and providing public and protected operations for use by other classes is the essence of encapsulation and information hiding in C++.

As an example, consider the data members of the Lendable class just described, particularly the way Jim has chosen to store the due date and borrower information in a nested class. The dueDate and borrowerID values will only be set by Lendable during check in and check out. No other class can arbitrarily change that data. And Jim can change the representation of Lendable without affecting any code other than the implementation of these functions because he knows that no code depends on the data members themselves, only the operations that manipulate them. Thus the notion of private state protects the Lendable code from other classes and protects other classes from changes to the Lendable code.

---

[4]Recall that although a static data member appears within the scope of the class, there is only one copy of the variable in the program.

[5]Recall that private members of a class are only accessible to the class itself and to functions and classes declared to be friends of the class.

Choosing C++ Member Functions

In this section, we decide upon the set of appropriate functions for a class and assign each an accessibility level. The set of member functions will encompass operations represented by CRC card design responsibilities. Functions that appear in every well-defined C++ class, such as constructors, a destructor, and certain operator functions, also need to be part of the class interface. We will consider these first, then examine design responsibilities.

CONSTRUCTORS

A *constructor* for a class defines how objects of that class will be created. A constructor is called by the compiler whenever an object of the class is declared or is created on the heap with operator new. Each class should have at least one constructor that will be used to initialize the data members of the object upon creation. There will be one constructor for each type of initializer for the class. For example, the Librarian class will probably just have a default constructor,[6] whereas a CheckIn class will have a constructor that takes a Borrower and a String (holding a lendable ID) for initialization. The implementation of the constructors will be influenced by the contents of *create* responsibilities, which signal work that needs to be done at creation time. For details on this, see the Member Function Implementation section.

Borrower and Lendable will each have at least one constructor that DB uses to create and initialize objects of these classes. Remember that no object of type Lendable will ever be created. But it still needs to declare a constructor that every Book, Video, and Journal object will use to initialize its Lendable base part.

DESTRUCTOR

The destructor for a class, if it exists, is called by the compiler whenever an object of that class goes out of scope or is destroyed with operator delete. There is one destructor call for each call to a constructor.

A programmer should define a destructor whenever any of its functions does something during the lifetime of an object that needs to be undone when the object is destroyed. Again, the most common example of destructor activity is memory deallocation,

---

[6]Recall that a default constructor has no arguments and is used to construct an object that is declared without an initializer.

but it may include closing files, disconnecting from database systems, or freeing of other system resources. A destructor may also print debugging information or update object counts. For example, the Librarian destructor (~Librarian()) might print a message "Goodnight. See you tomorrow." to show that system shut-down went smoothly.

All base classes should have destructors, and these destructors should be specified as virtual. We will cover this topic in more detail when we discuss the virtual specifier.

At this point there is no reason to believe that Borrower will need a destructor. The objects it will create as members can all destroy themselves reasonably. And no other resource allocation is done at creation time. This decision may change later if a member function is implemented to do something that needs to be undone when a Borrower object is destroyed.

The Lendable class, on the other hand, will need to define a destructor for two reasons. Lendable will make a call to new to create an OutRecord object in at least one of its constructors and as it checks itself out. Therefore, it will need a destructor that can delete the space if necessary. Also, since Lendable is a base class, it *must* have a destructor. Later we will declare it to be virtual.

COPY CONSTRUCTOR

A copy constructor for class Thing, usually Thing::Thing(const Thing&), tells the compiler how to initialize one object of type Thing from the value of another Thing object. It also determines how a Thing object is copied when it is passed as a function argument. Because this operation is so fundamental, the existence of a copy constructor is mandatory. If the programmer of class Thing does not provide an explicit copy constructor, the compiler will create one (called the *default copy constructor*) for use in the situations mentioned above. Each time a class is implemented, the author must determine whether this compiler-generated copy constructor does the right thing.

The default copy constructor is defined to do a member by member copy. For each data member of Thing that is a class object, e.g., Mem m, it calls Mem's copy constructor on that member (which in turn may need to be created by the compiler). In other words, it will recursively call copy constructors for its member class objects. For the remaining data members of Thing, a bitwise copy is performed. If Thing is derived from another class, e.g., Base, the default copy constructor copies the Base part of the Thing object by using the copy constructor for class Base.

There is no hard and fast rule for when a user-defined copy constructor is needed. In general, though, the definition of an explicit copy constructor is necessary when the class contains a pointer member, particularly if space is allocated for that member in a constructor and deleted in a destructor. Doing bitwise copies on pointers only copies the pointer and not what is pointed to. This can lead to disaster when the pointed-to thing is deleted by one of the objects.

Cecilia will not declare a copy constructor for class Borrower. Again, each of the member object types provides a copy constructor, so a memberwise copy will do the correct thing. On the other hand, Jim will declare a copy constructor for the Lendable class. He decides this by looking ahead to what will happen in his constructors and some of his responsibilities. For instance, he knows that his constructor and *check out* responsibility will create a new'ed object of his OutRecord class and assign it to his pointer member, out. Copies of Lendable objects need to include what out points to as well as out itself. Again, remember that no objects of type Lendable will exist explicitly, but copy constructors created by the compiler for the derived classes, Book, Video, and Journal, will use the Lendable copy constructor to copy the base class portion of these objects.

Even if a programmer cannot imagine that objects of the class will ever be copied, a copy constructor should be declared in cases where the default copy constructor is insufficient. By doing so, disaster can be averted if later the class is used in new ways. At the very least, if objects of a class are not meant to be copied, e.g., they are too large to be copied efficiently, the copy constructor should be declared as private. This will suppress the compiler generation of a copy constructor and cause an error if a copy is ever attempted.

ASSIGNMENT OPERATOR

An assignment operator for a class, say Thing, tells the compiler how to assign the value of a Thing object to an existing object of type Thing. Because this operation is so fundamental, the existence of an assignment operator is mandatory. If the programmer of class Thing does not provide an explicit assignment operator, the compiler will create one to do these assignments on a member by member basis. This default version is created even if Thing is derived from a class that defines an assignment operator, since assignment operators are not inherited.

For each data member of Thing that is a class object, e.g., of Mem m, the compiler calls Mem's assignment operator on that member. In other words, it will recursively call assignment operators for its member class objects. For the remaining data members of Thing, a bitwise assignment is performed. If Thing is derived from a class, Base, which has an explicit assignment operator, Base::operator=() is called to assign to the base class members.

Each time a class is implemented, the author must determine whether this compiler-generated assignment operator does the right thing. In general, if you need to define a copy constructor, you probably need to define an assignment operator. Therefore, Borrower will not declare an assignment operator, but Lendable will.

We will discuss issues in the signature of the assignment operator in the Member Function Signatures section. And we will talk about what needs to go inside each assignment operator when we get to the section on Member Function Implementation.

ACCESSOR/MUTATOR FUNCTIONS

A *know* responsibility in a design class reflects the fact that some class needs to know about, or change, an element of the state. Any such responsibility may have an associated C++ member function to retrieve this information, a member function to update the information, or both. Attributes, even without associated *know* responsibilities, may signal the need for these functions as well. Such functions are called *accessor* and *mutator* functions, respectively. Accessor and/or mutator functions should always be used by other classes (even derived classes) to interact with the class state.

Conventions for naming accessor and mutator functions vary. Some people advocate the use of get and set prefixes for the names of the functions. We find that accessor and mutator functions do more than simply get and set elements; therefore, more descriptive names are usually appropriate. We will not follow a particular convention. Each function will be given a name that is meaningful for how the information is requested or changed.

Borrower has two *know* responsibilities: *know number of lendables* and *know total fine*. The first question to ask is, "Who needs this information and what do they do with it?" The only client of the *know number of lendables* responsibility is Borrower itself as a subresponsibility of *can borrow*. Cecilia decides not to define an accessor function for Borrower's own use. Borrower also needs to *know total fine* as a subresponsibility of *can borrow*. But Cecilia remembers that this is also used by Check In to update the total fine information when Borrower returns an overdue item. So she declares a mutator function called addToTotalFine(), which will increment the total fine by some amount.

Borrower also has a name attribute with no corresponding *know* responsibility. Who needs to access or change this information? Certainly, DB will need to get it while storing a Borrower in the database, but Cecilia and Jim are leaning toward defining DB as a friend of their classes since it needs such intimate knowledge of their internals. Cecilia checks with Jim and Betty. Neither remember a specific use of this attribute, but Betty suggests that a class might use the name to personalize a message at some point. Cecilia decides to keep the attribute, but define no accessor or mutator function at this point.

Next, Jim looks at Lendable's *know* responsibilities to determine what accessor and mutator functions need to be added to the interface of the class. The first responsibility Jim looks at is *know borrower*. Only Lendable uses this responsibility to set its borrower information during check out. Jim opts not to declare a corresponding accessor or mutator function as a member of Lendable unless he discovers that someone else needs to retrieve or change that information.

Jim then considers the *know if overdue* responsibility. This is information needed by other classes, e.g., Borrower, when fulfilling the *can borrow* responsibility. Jim will declare a function called isOverdue() to answer this question. He will also declare an inOrOut() function corresponding to the *know in or out status* responsibility, which will check the value of the out pointer and let the caller know the status of the Lendable.

The *know due date* responsibility is only used by Lendable classes, but because the derived classes Book, Video, and Journal need the information,[7] Jim will declare a function to access it, called dueDate(). For the same reason, Jim declares a static member function, called todaysDate(), to access the today static member. This satisfies Lendable's newly added *know today's date* responsibility.

After exhausting the *know* responsibilities on the Lendable card, Jim peruses the attribute list and finds that lendable ID is unaccounted for. He wonders who needs this information. DB will need it to determine how to store the Lendable object in the database, but it won't need a function to do that, since DB will be a friend of Lendable. When Jim checks with Cecilia and Betty, Cecilia reminds him that she will need access to the lendable ID of the items on her list in order to find a particular lendable, given a lendable ID entered by the user during check in. So Jim adds a function called lendableId() to access this information.

OTHER FUNCTIONS

As we discussed in the Responsibilities section, some responsibilities correspond to lines in member functions (especially subresponsibilities), while others correspond to more than one member function. But some actually correspond fairly directly to one member function. Some of these are accessor and mutator functions. The rest of these need to be noted and declared next.

---

[7]Recall that a derived class cannot directly access private members of the base class.

Cecilia takes a look at the non-*know* responsibilities of Borrower that are needed by classes other than Borrower itself. The most prominent is *can borrow*, which she declares as a member function with the name canBorrow(). The *delete lendable from set* and *add lendable to set* responsibilities become deleteLendable() and addLendable() in Borrower's public interface. Although *retrieve lendable from set* is listed on the Borrower card as a subresponsibility of *can borrow*, Cecilia recalls that Check In also needs to use it to get the Book, Video, or Journal object that corresponds to the item being returned. So she declares a findLendable() function for public consumption.

Jim notices that Lendable has four non-*know* responsibilities, which can be represented by single member functions. He declares these as member functions with predictable names. The *check in* responsibility becomes the checkIn() function, and *check out* translates to checkOut(). He declares two functions for use by Lendable called calculateFine() and calculateDueDate(), corresponding to the *calculate fine* and *calculate due date* responsibilities.

ACCESSIBILITY

Each member function, as it is declared, is assigned an accessibility level that reflects which classes will need to use it. Functions that represent services requested by unrelated classes will be *public* member functions. Functions that represent responsibilities needed by derived classes will be declared *protected. Private* member functions will represent responsibilities used only by the class itself to implement the public and protected operations. In a class definition, the public interface is generally listed first, followed by the protected members, and finally the private functions and data.

BORROWER AND LENDABLE

The following are the skeletal declarations of the Borrower and Lendable classes. The correct signatures and function specifiers will be added in forthcoming sections.

Borrower has only public member functions and private data, as follows:

```
class Borrower {
public:
  Borrower();
  canBorrow();
  findLendable();
  deleteLendable();
  addLendable();
  addToTotalFine();
private:
```

```
        // private data
    };
```

A Lendable, because it is a base class, will have functions in the protected sections of its interface in addition to its public and private functions:

```
class Lendable {
public:
    Lendable();
    Lendable(const Lendable&); // copy constructor
    ~Lendable();
    operator=();
    lendableId();
    isOverdue();
    inOrOut();
    checkIn();
    checkOut();

protected:
    dueDate();
    static todaysDate();
private:
    calculateFine();
    calculateDueDate();
    // private data
};
```

This is simply a preliminary list of member functions. The need for new functions, such as operator functions, additional accessor and mutator functions, and private functions, may be discovered as the implementation of member functions takes place.

Member Function Signatures

The set of arguments of a C++ function is called its *signature*. The signature of a class member function, as well as its return type, will reflect the use of the function to fulfill a design-level collaboration. The arguments to the function will be the types of information that are sent with the message to a collaborating object. They represent information needed by the collaborator that is not global, local, or in the collaborator's state. Giving names to these arguments when declaring the function provides useful information to the user reading the class declaration.

The return type of the function will represent information that is expected by the initiator in response to the message it sends. Functions that simply provide a service often have a return type of void (or perhaps a type to contain status information). Other functions have a return type that reflects the type of information being requested. The following sections highlight the determination of return types and signatures for the various types of member functions.

CONSTRUCTOR AND DESTRUCTOR

Constructors and destructors do not have return types. And destructors do not have arguments; so their signatures are trivial to determine. The only work then is determining the arguments for the set of constructors. This is done by examining scenarios in which they are created. Borrower and Lendable objects are created by the DB object (in its getBorrower() and getLendable() functions) with data that has been retrieved from the database. For both of these classes the question is, how much of their state can be initialized by the class itself and how much needs to be initialized with data passed as arguments?

Borrower has two String members, borrowerID and name, one Money member, totalFine, and a TPtrSlist<Lendable> member called lendSet. Data to initialize the String and Money members will need to be passed to the constructor by DB, probably in the form of two char*'s and a double. But Borrower can create an empty TPtrSlist<Lendable> object itself. The List collaborator for Borrower's *create* responsibility confirms this. Then DB can populate this list by creating Lendable objects and using addLendable(). The following is the declaration of the Borrower constructor:

```
Borrower(
  const char* empID,    // employee ID
  const char* nm,       // name
  double fine           // total fine
);
```

As with Borrower, some of Lendable's members will be initialized with data from the database, e.g., lendableID and deweyDecimalNumber. But how about the OutRecord member and the dueDate and borrowerID members for an "out" Lendable? Jim decides that there will be two different constructors, one for an "in" Lendable, which initializes its out member to 0, and one for an "out" Lendable with two extra arguments that Lendable will use to create its OutRecord object. The following are the two constructor declarations:

```
Lendable(
  const char* lendID,    // lendable ID
  const char* ddn        // dewey decimal number
);
Lendable(
  const char*,lendID,    // lendable ID
  const char* ddn        // dewey decimal number
```

```
      const Date& ddate,       // due date
      const char* borrID       // borrower ID
);
```

COPY CONSTRUCTOR

A copy constructor has no return type (since it is a constructor) and takes a reference to the class as the argument. The reference can be to a const or nonconst object of the class, i.e., it can be Lendable(Lendable&) or Lendable(const Lendable&), but it *must* be a reference. A copy constructor with a nonreference argument type, e.g., Lendable(Lendable), will enter an infinite loop as soon as the first copy is attempted.[8]

ASSIGNMENT OPERATOR

Some beginner C++ programmers define their operator=() with a void return type. The problem with this scheme is that it does not support or allow for chained assignments, such as x=y=z. In order to mimic this capability of the assignment operator for built-in types, the user-defined operator=() should be defined with a return type that is a reference to the class. As we will see later, the function will return *this.

   Returning a nonconst reference to the assigned object causes the result of the assignment to be an lvalue and allows it to then be the left-hand side of another assignment as follows: (x=y) = z. This is counter to what is allowed with built-in types and can be avoided by defining the return type to be a reference to const, e.g.,

```
      const Lendable& operator=(const Lendable&);
```

ACCESSOR/MUTATOR FUNCTIONS

It is usually straightforward to assign a return type and signature to accessor and mutator functions. The return type of a mutator function is usually void,[9] and the argument list of an accessor is often (but not always) empty. The return type of an accessor is the type of the information it requests, and the argument list of a mutator is generally the type of a new value being used to update the information referred to by the name of the function.

   For example, users of Borrower's addToTotalFine() will pass a value (probably a double) to be used to increment Borrower's totalFine member. And Lendable's isOverdue(),

---

[8]Why? Because the constructor will be called repeatedly in an attempt to copy its own argument.

[9]Some type of status information to return the success or failure of the mutator function may also be useful as a return type.

because it asks a yes or no question, will return TRUE or FALSE, which has been defined in a Boolean enum type.

OTHER FUNCTIONS

In general, return types and signatures for functions in the class interface can be inferred by looking at typical uses of the function in a design scenario. For example, to determine the return type and signature of the canBorrow() member function, Cecilia will look at how it is used in a scenario. She remembers that Check Out asks Borrower to check and return its status as part of its *execute* responsibility. In essence, the CheckOut object will use this function to ask the Borrower "can you borrow?" Since CheckOut expects a yes or no answer, a Boolean type is appropriate as the return type. The argument list to canBorrow() should consist of the types of things that Borrower needs from CheckOut in order to fulfill this responsibility. But Borrower only needs to look at objects in its own state to determine its borrowability; therefore, the argument list for the function will be empty.

The Check In class relies on Borrower's *delete lendable from set* responsibility as part of its *execute* responsibility (when it updates the Borrower's set of lendables). This is simply a service that needs to be fulfilled; therefore, the return type for Borrower's delete-Lendable() function can be void. But what does Borrower need from Check In in order to delete a Lendable? It needs some indication of what Lendable should be taken out of the set. To determine the type, Cecilia looks ahead to the implementation. She refers to the documentation of the TPtrSlist class and finds a function:

```
T* remove(const T* a);
```

that removes the first element in the list that is equal to the argument, a. The test for equality is done with a user-provided operator==() function for T. So Cecilia decides that she will use this function as the implementation of deleteLendable(); thus, the right type for the argument is Lendable*. She informs Jim that Lendable needs to define a comparison operator, so Jim adds operator==() to Lendable's public interface.

As another example, Jim knows that Lendable's checkOut() function performs a service; thus he will define the return type as void. In order to determine the set of arguments, he examines a scenario where Check Out asks the Lendable to check itself out. How much of this can he do with his own knowledge, and what does he need from Check Out? He can calculate his own due date, but he needs the borrower information to be given to him. Therefore, Jim declares the checkOut() function with a String argument that represents the borrower ID.

BORROWER AND LENDABLE

Jim and Cecilia go through this exercise with each of Borrower's and Lendable's functions to determine a preliminary set of return types and signatures. The results of their efforts are shown below.

```
class Borrower {
  Borrower(
    const char* empID, const char* nm, double fine
  );
  Boolean canBorrow();
  void deleteLendable(Lendable* itsGone);
  void addLendable(Lendable* itsNew);
  void addToTotalFine(double more);
private:
  // private data
};
```

Note that Jim has decided to declare operator==() to be a friend[10] of Lendable rather than a member. He knows from his reading[7] that binary operators, other than assignment operators and compound assignment operators should be declared as friends. This allows conversions to take place on both arguments.

```
class Lendable {

public:
  Lendable(const char* lendID, const char* ddn);
  Lendable(
    const char* lendID,
    const char* ddn,
    const Date& ddate,
    const char* borrID
  );
  Lendable(const Lendable&); // copy constructor
  ~Lendable();
  const Lendable& operator=(const Lendable&);
  friend Boolean operator==(
    const Lendable& lhs, const Lendable& rhs
  );
  Boolean isOverdue();
  IOStatus inOrOut();

  void checkIn();

  void checkOut(const String& borrID);
```

---

[10]Recall that a friend function has access to the private members of a class.

```
protected:
  Date dueDate();
  static Date todaysDate();
private:
  double calculateFine();
  Date calculateDueDate();
  enum IOStatus { IN, OUT };
  // private data
};
```

These function declarations are still not complete, because they do not include specifiers such as inline, const, and virtual. The applicability of these modifiers will be determined in the next section.

Member Function Specifiers

At some point between declaring the member functions and defining their implementation (or as part of both), we decide on the appropriate specifiers to be part of the declarations and definitions.

CONST MEMBER FUNCTIONS

Declaring a member function to be *const* tells a user of the class that the function will not alter the state of the object. Thus, users can call the function on both const and nonconst objects of the class. Any call to a nonconst member function on a const object will elicit an error from the compiler.

Any member function that does not alter the values of any data member of the class should be declared const. This ensures that the function can be used on the widest range of objects. Not declaring a function const needlessly restricts the set of objects upon which it can be called. For example, accessor functions are generally const, e.g.,

```
class Lendable {
//...
  IOStatus inOrOut() const;
};

IOStatus
Lendable::inOrOut() const
{
  if (out==0) return Lendable::IN;
  else return Lendable::OUT;
}
```

The const keyword must appear in both the function declaration and in the function definition before the body of the function.

From a user's point of view, a function may not change the state of an object even if it modifies a member of the class internally for reasons known only to the class author. In these cases, this illusion of constness should be preserved for the user by declaring the function to be const and casting away constness inside the function where changes are made to these data members.[11]

For example, Jim implements the execute() member function of the CheckOut class to call Borrower's canBorrow() member function each time another Lendable is presented. This is necessary since the borrower's fine may have increased since the last lendable was checked out or the borrower may have surpassed their lendable limit. But Jim realizes that checking whether each existing Lendable in the Borrower's set is overdue should just be done once; and repeating this check for each Lendable is inefficient.

When Jim points this out to Cecilia, she agrees and decides to add a new integer member to Borrower, called noOverdue. The noOverdue flag is set to 0 in the constructor for a new Borrower object and is set to 1 in canBorrow() if no overdue Lendables are found. Later invocations of canBorrow() know not to check for overdue Lendables if this value is set.

The problem is that the canBorrow() member function is const from the user's point of view since it does not change the state of the Borrower. But it now needs to change a Borrower data member, which will cause the compiler to complain bitterly. So Cecilia declares it to be const and implements it with a cast as follows:

```
Boolean
Borrower::canBorrow() const
{
  if (totalFine > 100.00) return FALSE;
  if (lendSet.entries() == 5) return FALSE;
  if (noOverdue == 1) return TRUE;
  for (int i=0;i<lendSet.entries();i++) {
    Lendable* lp = lendSet.at(i);
    if (lp->isOverdue()) {
      return FALSE;
    }
  }
  ((Borrower*)this)->noOverdue = 1;
  return TRUE;
}
```

---

[11]This is the *only* situation in which casting away const is considered appropriate.

This function can now be called on const and nonconst Borrower objects.

INLINE SPECIFIER

In C++, when a function is declared to be *inline*, the programmer is asking the compiler to expand the contents of the function inline, thus avoiding the cost of an actual function call. The fact that the compiler will do this is the reason C++ can efficiently implement the concepts of encapsulation and information hiding. The fact that the compiler will sometimes ignore this request can lead to code bloat and less efficient programs.

The goal is to use inline for functions where performance is critical, but not to run the risk of "outlined inlines."[12] Simple accessor and mutator functions are the most common candidates to be inline functions, but inlining can be used for any very small (1- or 2-line) function. The inline keyword must be used in the definition of the function and may optionally be included in the function's declaration as well.

For example, the checkIn() and checkOut() functions of Lendable, though not accessors or mutators, are short enough to be reasonable candidates for inline functions.

```
inline void
Lendable::checkIn()
{
   delete out;
   out = 0;
}
inline void
Lendable::checkOut(const String& borrID)
{
   out = new OutRecord(calculateDueDate(),borrID);
}
```

As Jim implements checkOut(), he realizes that he needs a constructor for OutRecord to initialize its members, so he adds that to his Lendable class.

VIRTUAL SPECIFIER

Inheritance and *virtual* functions are one way that C++ implements the notion of polymorphism described in Chapter 1 (see the Superclass/Subclass Relationships section). In design, some responsibilities were listed on a superclass CRC card and listed again on the

---

[12]These are static versions of inline functions, which the compiler creates in each file that calls the function, usually unbeknownst to the programmer. They cause code size increases without the accompanying gain in efficiency.

cards of each of the subclasses. This implied that the responsibility would be carried out differently by objects of each of the subclasses. Functions that correspond to these responsibilities are the ones that should be declared virtual. The functions that correspond to responsibilities listed only on the superclass card do not need to be declared virtual.

For example, the behavior of the *execute* responsibility of the Transaction class depends upon which type of transaction is actually being executed. In the implementation, variables can be defined with type Transaction*[13] but actually be initialized with new CheckOut, CheckIn, or Search objects. Functions defined to be virtual in the base class, i.e., execute() and ~Transaction(), and uniquely redefined on derived classes can be called through the Transaction pointers, and the behavior will be appropriate for the type of the actual object. For example, the following is the Transaction class declaration and the transaction loop of Librarian's waitForUser() function.

```
class Transaction {
// ...
public:
  Transaction(Borrower*);
  virtual ~Transaction();
  virtual void execute();
};

void
Librarian::waitForUser()
{
  // ...
  Action todo;
  Transaction *trans;
  while((todo=user.getAction()) != Librarian::EXIT) {
    switch (todo) {
      case CHECKOUT:
        String lendID = user.getLendableId();
        trans = new CheckOut(currBorr, lendID);
        break;
      case CHECKIN:
        String lendID = user.getLendableId();
        trans = new CheckIn(currBorr, lendID);
        break;
      case SEARCH:
        trans = new Search(currBorr);
        break;
      default:
```

---

[13]They can also be of type Transaction&, but we will use pointers in this discussion for simplicity.

```
            user.displayMessage("Illegal Option");
            continue;
        }
        trans->execute();
        delete trans;
    }
}
```

The fact that execute() is declared to be virtual ensures that the trans->execute() statement will be carried out correctly, though very differently, depending on the type of Transaction. The virtual destructor in Transaction will be empty, but its existence tells the compiler to call the appropriate derived class destructor even when the object is being deleted through the base class pointer.

The following is the portion of the Lendable interface that is declared to be virtual.

```
class Lendable {
    //...
    virtual Date calculateDueDate() const = 0;
    virtual double calculateFine() const = 0;
    virtual ~Lendable();
};
```

First note that Lendable is given a virtual destructor. Classes derived from Lendable may, at some point, need to define a destructor of their own. A virtual destructor in the base class guarantees that the derived class destructor will be called when a derived class object is destroyed through a base class pointer. The destructor will be defined as follows:

```
Lendable::~Lendable()
{
    delete out;
}
```

Notice that the virtual keyword is just an attribute of the declaration of the function. It is not repeated in the definition. Also, notice that Jim has resisted the temptation to declare ~Lendable(), a very short function, as inline. Virtual functions should not be inline. Because of their implementation in C++, the address of the virtual functions needs to be stored; thus, copies of those functions are always created. In addition, any call of a virtual function through a base class pointer will not be expanded inline.

The calculateFine() and calculateDueDate() functions are also declared to be virtual because their implementations will depend on whether the object is a Book, Video, or Journal. The remainder of the operations will be implemented in the same way for all Lendables; therefore the functions inherited by subclasses will suffice. Note that calculateFine() and calculateDueDate() are initialized to 0 in the class declaration. This declares them to be *pure* as well as virtual. Declaring a pure virtual member function tells the compiler that Lendable is an abstract base class and ensures that no instances of this class can be created. It also frees Jim from having to provide a base class definition of these functions.

Let's look at the implementation of these functions in a derived class, Video. Note that the virtual keyword does not need to be repeated in the derived class declaration of the function. But the return type and signature of the function must match that of the base class version exactly. Remember that a video is borrowed for 1 week, and an overdue video costs $5 per day.

```
class Video : public Lendable {
//...
public:
//...
  Date calculateDueDate() const;
  double calculateFine() const;
};

Date
Video::calculateDueDate() const
{
  return todaysDate() + 7;
}

double
Video::calculateFine() const
{
  if (todaysDate() <= dueDate()) {
    return 0.0;
  }
  return (todaysDate() - dueDate()) * 5.0;
}
```

Member Function Implementation

The final step in defining a C++ class is the actual implementation of the member functions. At this point, a preliminary interface for each class has been developed and shared with every member of the team. Therefore, Jim and Cecilia are each aware of the set of functions at their disposal while detailing the working of their functions in C++. Implementors rely on these interfaces, their familiarity with the design, the information on the CRC cards, and the documentation of scenarios to do their job.

We will look at this process in more detail soon, but first we examine the implementation aspects of the special C++ class functions.

CONSTRUCTORS

The implementation of a constructor consists primarily of initializing the data members of the class. When an object is declared and the appropriate constructor called, each data member is first initialized and then the body of the constructor is executed. A programmer can provide an *initialization list* before the body of the constructor, in which members are paired with values used during the initialization phase.

Therefore, there are two ways for the constructor to give a data member a value at the time of object construction. The member can be initialized in an initialization list, or it can be assigned to in the body of the constructor. In general, the initialization list should be used. For some types of members, the initialization syntax is the only legal way to obtain a value. In other cases, it is the more efficient alternative.

For example, const and reference variables are initialized as they are created and can never be assigned to. Therefore, members of these types must be given a value in an initialization list. For instance, the Call class must initialize its two reference members as follows:

```
Call::Call(Telephone& t1, Telephone& t2)
: caller(t1), callee(t2)     // initialization list
{ }
```

The initializer must also be used for members that are objects of classes without a default constructor. If a data member that is itself a class object (say, of type Mem) is assigned inside a constructor, e.g.,

```
class Mem { private: int i; public Mem(int); };
class Thing { private: Mem x; public: Thing(int)};

Thing::Thing(int i) { x = i; };
```

the Thing constructor will first try to call the default constructor for Mem (Mem::Mem()), then the assignment operator for Mem. This will elicit an error from the compiler since no default constructor exists for Mem.[14] In this case, the only way to initialize the Mem member is to give it a value in an initializer list.

---

[14]Recall that the compiler will only create a default constructor for a class that defines no constructors of its own.

Assigning to a class object within a constructor is also less efficient than using an initializer list because two functions are called instead of one. For instance, let us look at a version of the Borrower constructor that assigns to its members inside the function.

```
Borrower::Borrower(const char* id, const char* n, double f)
{
  borrowerID = id;
  name = n;
  totalFine = f;
  noOverdue = 0;
}
```

The construction of each Borrower object will require six function calls. There will be two calls to String::String() and one call to Money::Money() during initialization, and then three calls to assignment operators in the body of the function. The following implementation using an initialization list

```
Borrower::Borrower(
  const char* id, const char* n, double f
)
: borrowerID(id), name(n), totalFine(f), noOverdue(0)
{ }
```

will require just three function calls. There will be two calls to String::String(const char*) and one to Money::Money(double).

Since base class members cannot be directly accessed by derived classes, a base class must also be initialized in an initialization list whenever arguments are necessary for its construction. For example, here is one of the Lendable constructors with its corresponding Book constructor.

```
Lendable::Lendable(const char* id, const char* dd)
: lendableID(id), deweyDecimalNumber(dd)
{ }

Book::Book(
  const char* id, const char* dd, const char* t,
  const char* au, const char* pub, const Date& pdate
)
: Lendable(id, dd), title(t), author(au), publisher(pub),
  pubDate(pdate)
{ }
```

In C++, data members of a class are initialized in the order they are declared, not in the order they are listed in the initialization list. The effects of this are normally transparent, but it can cause problems in cases where a data member is initialized using the value of another member. It is safest to simply list the items in an initialization list in declaration order.

To aid in the implementation of the constructor, the class implementor should look at the CRC card for any *create* responsibilities to determine what else needs to get done at creation time. For example, Check In's *create* responsibility lists the Borrower and DB classes as collaborators. Cecilia remembers from the design sessions, and sees in the scenario tables, that upon creation, Check In either (1) gets the current lendable from the current Borrower or (2) gets a new Borrower from DB and gets the current Lendable from that. She implements the constructor accordingly.

```
CheckIn::CheckIn(Borrower* bp, const String& lendID)
: Transaction(bp), diffBorrower(0)
{
  currLend = currBorr->findLendable(lendID);
  if(!currLend) {
    currBorr = db.getBorrowerWithLendId(lendID);
    currLend = currBorr->findLendable(lendID);
    diffBorrower = 1;
  }
}
```

DESTRUCTOR

The destructor exists to undo whatever has been done in the course of an object's lifetime. Hints for the body of a destructor come mostly from the implementation of the constructors and other functions. If a new appears in a function, a delete had better be part of the destructor. If a file or connection to a database is opened somewhere along the line, it should be closed in the destructor.

Sometimes, *destroy* responsibilities are actually written on cards with collaborators that provide input into the implementation of the destructor. For example, here is the destructor for the CheckIn class that corresponds to its *destroy* responsibility.

```
CheckIn::~CheckIn()
{
  db.putLendable(currLend);
  if (diffBorrower) db.putBorrower(currBorr);
}
```

ASSIGNMENT OPERATOR

In general, the implementation of the assignment operator involves deleting the contents of the object being assigned to, then copying the contents of the argument into that existing object. For example, the Lendable assignment operator might perform these steps as follows:

```
const Lendable&
Lendable::operator=(const Lendable& s)
{
   delete out;
   lendableID = s.lendableID;
   deweyDecimalNumber = s.deweyDecimalNumber;
   out = new OutRecord(s.out->dueDate,s.out->borrowerID);
   return *this;
}
```

But imagine that the argument, s, is really just another name for the Lendable being assigned to. When we delete the memory associated with out, we are actually deleting s.out, the memory associated with the argument from which we hope to copy. If that memory is reallocated and reused before the OutRecord copy is done, the new Lendable will have a garbage value.

Therefore, the first statement of each assignment operator should be the following check to determine if the right-hand side of the assignment expression is really the same as the object being assigned to:

```
if (&s == this) return *this;
```

Another implementation issue associated with the assignment operator is the assignment of base class elements. Suppose you wish to define your own assignment operator for the KnightMare class as part of the implementation of a new Chess game. KnightMare is derived from the class ChessPiece, which defines its own assignment operator. If you wish to use ChessPiece's assignment operator to assign to the ChessPiece members of the KnightMare object, you must explicitly call it from within KnightMare's assignment operator as follows:

```
const KnightMare&
KnightMare::operator=(const KnightMare& km)
{
   if (&km == this) return *this;

   ((ChessPiece&) *this) = km;
```

```
   // KnightMare assignment
   return *this;
}
```

ACCESSOR/MUTATOR FUNCTIONS

The implementation of accessor and mutator functions are usually fairly simple. Accessor functions are defined to return some piece of the object's state which has been either stored or can be quickly calculated. Mutator functions set or update the object's state.

Because the body of these functions are generally so small, they are usually declared to be inline. For example, Lendable's function that returns the due date information for an "out" Lendable is defined as follows:

```
inline Date
Lendable::dueDate() const
{
   return out->dueDate;
}
```

And Borrower's addToTotalFine() mutator function will also be defined as inline.

```
inline void
Borrower::addToTotalFine(double d)
{
   totalFine += d;
}
```

OTHER FUNCTIONS

The process of implementing most member functions should be fairly straightforward. Collaborators, combined with the scenario documentation, provide a developer with an outline of how responsibilities are fulfilled. Implementation means detailing in C++ each step of the member function. It often includes adding error-handling code that is not explicitly defined by the CRC cards. Although we begin with a set of functions at our disposal, the actual implementation can uncover the need for new functions or changes to existing ones.

For example, Figure 6.4 shows the Check Out CRC card and a list of subresponsibilities for its *create, execute,* and *destroy* responsibilities. In this case, subresponsibilities provide a fairly detailed skeleton of each member function implementation. But knowledge of the design by the implementor, over and above what is on the cards, is still necessary

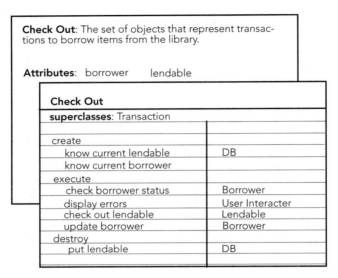

Figure 6.4 Check Out CRC card.

for the C++ implementation. For instance, the following is the final implementation of Jim's execute() function.

```
void CheckOut::execute()
{
  String msg;
  if (currBorr->canBorrow(msg)==FALSE) {
    user.displayMessage(msg);
    return;
  }
  if (!currLend) {
    user.displayMessage("Bad lendable ID");
    return;
  }
  if (currLend->inOrOut() == Lendable::OUT) {
    user.displayMessage(
      "That item is already checked out!"
    );
    return;
  }
  lp->checkOut(currBorr->borrowerId());
  currBorr->addLendable(currLend);
}
```

Although the CRC card listed *display errors* as a subresponsibility of *execute*, Jim has used his design and C++ knowledge to implement this error handling more explicitly. Also, Jim notices two changes to Borrower that he needs for an effective implementation. First, when he checks the borrower's status, he wants to elicit an error message if canBorrow() returns FALSE. But he would like to be fairly specific about the problem. He asks Cecilia to add a String& argument to her canBorrow() function, which, in case of a problem, is assigned a message detailing the reason the user cannot borrow. Finally, as Jim writes the C++ statement to *check out lendable*, he realizes that he has no way to get the borrower ID from the current borrower to use as the argument to checkOut(). So Cecilia adds a borrowerId() accessor function to Borrower's public interface. (See the Appendix for the implementation of the Borrower and Lendable member functions.)

Library Application

Cecilia and Jim work through the implementation of their classes, reconvening to negotiate changes and to review each other's code. They write unit tests for their classes based on scenario diagrams to verify that their implementation does not violate their design assumptions. As the system becomes usable, Betty begins to do some system testing. As they wind down the implementation and testing of the original application, Cecilia and Jim begin sessions with Dewey and Betty to model some of the other functions of the library, such as adding and deleting borrower and library material records and printing overdue notices.

C++ File Organization

Years of programming experience have resulted in a set of widely accepted conventions for the organization of C++ programs across files. C++ class declarations and their implementations are stored in two kinds of files: class header files and class source files.

Class Header Files

The class header file contains the declarations that will be needed by a user of a class. This includes the declarations of closely related classes and their associated data members, member functions, and friend functions. Any related const definitions and extern declarations should also be included in the header file.

Also, since inline functions are only known within the file in which they are defined, they need to be included in every source file that uses them. Therefore, the header file needs to include definitions of the class inline member and friend functions. The header file should *not* include any noninline function definitions.

The header file should have a ".h" extension and should be named for the most important class declared within. For example, Lendable.h will declare class Lendable and all of its derived classes and members.

A class declaration is also a definition in C++. Therefore, if a header file is included in a source file more than once, errors in the form of multiple definitions of the class will result. There will also be multiple definitions of any inline functions that are defined in the header file. This problem is avoided by putting preprocessor guards around header files to prevent the contents of a file from being included more than once. The preprocessor variable name varies. We use CLASSNAME_H, as in the following, to guard the entrance of the Borrower.h file.

```
#ifndef BORROWER_H
#define BORROWER_H

// header file contents

#endif
```

The most important part of the class header file is the class declaration. There are conventions for the organization of this declaration that make it easier for users to read and understand. Public declarations are always presented first since a reader tends to care most about the public interface. The protected members come next for readers who may want to derive from this class. Lastly comes the private part of the class.

Programmers should resist the temptation to define inline functions within the class definition. Defining them outside and immediately following the class separates the declaration of the class from implementation details. Remember that the inline keyword is always used for these definitions.

If an object of another class, say Foo, is used in the class header file, i.e., sent a message in an inline function definition, declared as a member of a class, or declared as an argument to a function, then Foo.h must be #included by the class header file. However, if only a pointer or reference to a Foo is mentioned, a forward declaration of Foo, i.e., class Foo;, should be used instead. This will reduce the size of the files that include the class header file, and they will not have to be recompiled whenever Foo.h changes.

For example, in Borrower.h a Lendable* is mentioned in the lendSet member of Borrower. So a forward reference to Lendable has been placed in Borrower.h to tell the compiler that Lendable is a class. This will make the Library application smaller and faster to compile than if it had #included Lendable.h.

```
#ifndef BORROWER_H
#define BORROWER_H

class Lendable;
class Borrower {
// ...
};

#endif
```

Class Source Files

A class source file contains the implementation of a class. Generally, all noninline member function definitions for classes declared in a single class header file are placed in one ".c" file named for the most important class, e.g., Borrower.c. The source file will also contain initializations of any static members.

If a given source file contains many member functions and only a few of these will be used in a typical application, then the file should be split, often one source file per member function. For example, class libraries are packaged this way to ensure that applications using them are as small as possible. Even when this split will ultimately occur, it is a good idea to keep one source file for development and split it only later for production use.

The source file must #include the corresponding class header file and any other header files that declare functions used by the implementation. Note that in Borrower.c, Lendable.h must be #included because member functions of Lendable will be used in the implementation of the Borrower class, e.g., isOverdue() in canBorrow().

Remember the Main

We claimed at the beginning of this chapter that developing an object-oriented application in C++ meant defining a set of C++ classes. While defining classes is the bulk of the development activity, it is also necessary to write a C++ main() routine to do setup and to start the application rolling. The following is the Library application main() routine.

```
#include "library.h"
#include "UserInteracter.h"
#include "DB.h"
#include "Librarian.h"

UserInteracter user;
DB db;

int
main()
{
   Librarian betty;
   betty.waitForUser();
}
```

Summing Up

Building a C++ prototype from a CRC card design requires a solid understanding of the design and how design elements are best represented in C++ language constructs. It also requires knowledge of the effective use of C++ when building classes.

    C++ classes are built from CRC card classes by naming and declaring the class from each card then implementing the class using CRC card design elements. Attributes, *know* responsibilities and **has-a** collaborations help determine the physical representation of the class. A set of member functions are formed by knowing what functions belong in a canonical C++ class and adding functions that encompass the responsibilities listed on the card. Return types, signatures, and implementations of functions are determined by looking at subresponsibilities, collaborations, and scenarios.

Coming Up

The Appendix contains the complete set of class declarations and member function implementations for the Borrower class and the Lendable hierarchy.

References

1. Budd, Timothy. *Introduction to Object-Oriented Programming*, Addison-Wesley, Reading, MA, 1991, p. 2. Reprinted by permission of the publisher.

2. Ellis, M. A., and Bjarne Stroustrup. *The Annotated C++ Reference Manual*, Addison-Wesley, Reading, MA, 1990.

3. Kernighan, Brian, and Dennis Ritchie. *The C Programming Language*, Addison-Wesley, Reading, MA, 1978.

4. Birtwistle, G. M., O.-J. Dahl, B. Myrhaug, and K. Nygaard. *Simula Begin*, 2nd ed. Studentlitteratur, Lund, 1979.

5. Lippman, Stanley. *C++ Primer*, 2nd ed. Addison-Wesley, Reading, MA, 1992.

6. Stroustrup, Bjarne. *The C++ Programming Language.* Addison-Wesley, Reading, MA, 1993.

7. Murray, Robert. *C++ Strategies and Tactics.* Addison-Wesley, Reading, MA, 1993.

8. Meyers, Scott. *Effective C++.* Addison-Wesley, Reading, MA, 1993.

9. Jacobson, Ivar, Magnus Christerson, Patrik Jonsson, and Gunnar Overgaard. *Object-Oriented Software Engineering.* Addison-Wesley, Reading, MA, 1992.

CRC to C++

It is a long road from the inception of a thing

to its realization.

—Molière, *Le Tartuffe*, act 3, scene 1

IN CHAPTER 6, we discussed the issues involved in moving a CRC card design to an effective implementation in C++. Here we show the complete realization of that translation for the Borrower class and each class in the lendable hierarchy. The CRC cards from the design sessions are reproduced here for comparison to the C++ code that implements it.

Borrower Card

Figure A.1 shows the Borrower CRC card that Cecilia created in the design sessions.

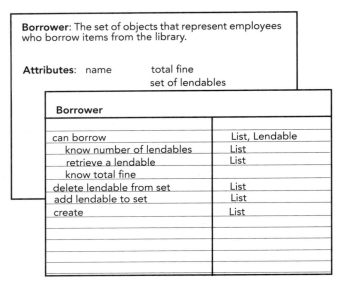

Figure A.1. Borrower CRC card

Borrower.h

```
/*****************************************************
* Library Application: Borrower class declaration
*
* The Borrower class defines the set of objects
* that represent users who borrow items from the
* library
*
* Author: Cecilia
*****************************************************/
#ifndef BORROWER_H
#define BORROWER_H

#include "library.h"
#include <RWTPtrSlist.h>
#include <RWMoney.h>
#include <String.h>

class Lendable;

class Borrower {
public:
```

```
    Borrower(
       const char* empID, const char* nm, double fine
    );
    void addLendable(Lendable*);
    void deleteLendable(const Lendable*);
    Lendable* findLendable(const String&);
    Boolean canBorrow(String& errmsg) const;
    void addTotalFine(double);
    String borrowerId() const;
private:
    int noOverdue;
    String borrowerID;
    String name;
    RWMoney totalFine;
    RWTPtrSlist<Lendable> lendSet;
    friend class DB;
};

inline void
Borrower::addTotalFine(double d)
{
    totalFine += d;
}

inline String
Borrower::borrowerId() const
{
    return borrowerID;
}

#endif
```

Borrower.c

```
/**************************************************
* Library Application: Borrower implementation
*
* Author: Cecilia
**************************************************/

#include "library.h"
#include "Borrower.h"
#include <String.h>
#include "Lendable.h"

Borrower::Borrower(
```

```
      const char* empID,
      const char* nm,
      double fine
)
: borrowerID(empID), name(nm), totalFine(fine), noOverdue(0)
{ }

void
Borrower::addLendable(Lendable* lp)
{
   lendSet.append(lp);
}

Boolean
Borrower::canBorrow(String& msg) const
{
   if (totalFine > 100.0) {
     msg = "Over the $100 fine limit!";
     return FALSE;
   }

   if (lendSet.entries() >= 5) {
     msg = "Too many items out!";
     return FALSE;
   }

   if (noOverdue == 1) return TRUE;

   for (int i=0; i< lendSet.entries(); i++) {
     Lendable* lp = lendSet.at(i);
     if (lp->isOverdue()) {
        msg = "Overdue item!";
        return FALSE;
     }
   }

   ((Borrower*)this)->noOverdue = 1;
   return TRUE;
}

void
Borrower::deleteLendable(const Lendable* lend)
{
   (void) lendSet.remove(lend);
}
```

```
Lendable*
Borrower::findLendable(const String& lendID)
{
   for (int i=0; i< lendSet.entries(); i++) {
     Lendable* lp = lendSet.at(i);
     if (lp->lendableId() == lendID) {
       return lp;
     }
   }
   return 0;
}
```

Lendable Card

Figure A.2 shows the Lendable CRC card that Jim created in the design sessions. Figure A.3 shows the CRC card that Jim created in the design sessions for the classes derived from Lendable: Book, Video, and Journal. The definitions of the C++ classes corresponding to these cards will be stored in Lendable.h along with the declaration of their base class, Lendable.

Lendable.h

```
/****************************************************
 * Library Application:
 * Lendable class hierarchy declarations
 *
 * Lendable defines the set of objects that repre-
 * sent items to be borrowed from the library
 *
 * Subclasses: Book, Video, Journal
 *
 * Author: Jim
 ****************************************************/

#ifndef LENDABLE_H
#define LENDABLE_H
```

```
#include <RWDate.h>
#include <String.h>

class Lendable {
public:
   enum IOStatus { OUT, IN };
   Lendable(const char* lendID, const char* ddn);
   Lendable(
      const char* lendID,
      const char* ddn,
      const RWDate& ddate,
      const char* borrID
   );
   Lendable(const Lendable&);
   const Lendable& operator=(const Lendable&);
   virtual ~Lendable();
   String lendableId() const;
   friend int operator==(
      const Lendable& lhs, const Lendable& rhs
   );
```

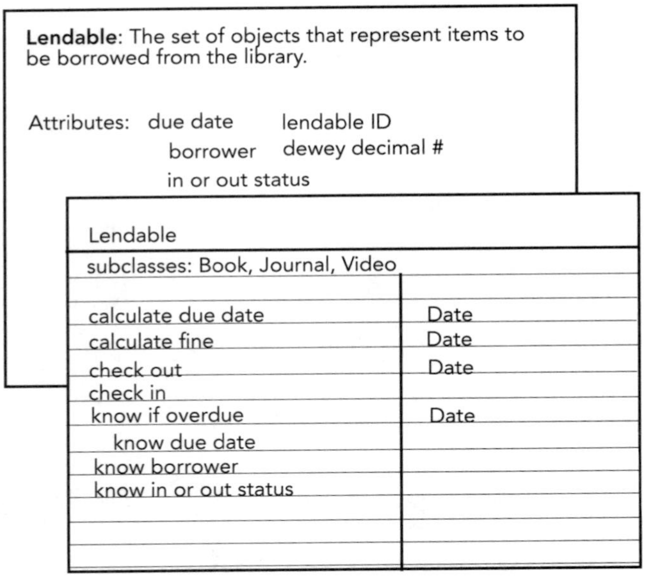

Lendable: The set of objects that represent items to be borrowed from the library.

Attributes:	due date	lendable ID
	borrower	dewey decimal #
	in or out status	

Lendable	
subclasses: Book, Journal, Video	
calculate due date	Date
calculate fine	Date
check out	Date
check in	
know if overdue	Date
know due date	
know borrower	
know in or out status	

Figure A.2. Lendable CRC card.

Book: The set of objects that represent books to be borrowed from the library.

Attributes: title   publisher
           author publication date

Book	
superclass: Lendable	
calculate due date	Date
calculate fine	Date

Video: The set of objects that represent videos to be borrowed from the library.

Attributes: title   date
           producer vhs or beta

Video	
superclass: Lendable	
calculate due date	Date
calculate fine	Date

Journal: The set of objects that represent journals to be borrowed from the library.

Attributes: title   date
           volume issue

Journal	
superclass: Lendable	
calculate due date	Date
calculate fine	Date

Figure A.3. Book, Video, and Journal CRC cards.

```
     IOStatus inOrOut() const;
     int isOverdue() const;
     double checkIn();
     void checkOut(const String& borrID);
protected:
     RWDate dueDate() const;
     static RWDate todaysDate();
private:
     static RWDate today;
     String lendableID;
     String deweyDecimalNumber;
     class OutRecord {
     public:
       OutRecord(const RWDate& d, const char* b)
         : dueDate(d), borrowerID(b) { }
       RWDate dueDate;
       String borrowerID;
     };
     OutRecord* out;
     virtual double calculateFine() const = 0;
     virtual RWDate calculateDueDate() const = 0;
     friend class DB;
};

inline String
Lendable::lendableId() const
{
   return lendableID;
}

inline Lendable::IOStatus
Lendable::inOrOut() const
{
   if (out) return Lendable::OUT;
   else return Lendable::IN;
}

inline RWDate
Lendable::dueDate() const
{
   return out->dueDate;
}

inline RWDate
Lendable::todaysDate()
{
   return today;
}
```

```
inline int
operator==(const Lendable& l1, const Lendable& l2)
{
   return (l1.lendableID == l2.lendableID);
}

class Book : public Lendable {
private:
   String title;
   String author;
   String publisher;
   RWDate pubDate;
   double calculateFine() const;
   RWDate calculateDueDate() const;
public:
   Book(
      const char* lendID,
      const char* ddn,
      const char* t,
      const char* au,
      const char* pub,
      const RWDate& pdate
   );
   Book(
      const char* lendID,
      const char* ddn,
      const RWDate& ddate,
      const char* borrID,
      const char* t,
      const char* au,
      const char* pub,
      const RWDate& pdate
   );
};

class Video : public Lendable {
private:
   String title;
   String producer;
   enum mode { VHS, BETA } vhsOrBeta;
   RWDate relDate;
   double calculateFine() const;
   RWDate calculateDueDate() const;
public:
   Video(
      const char* lendID,
      const char* ddn,
      const char* t,
```

```
      const char* pro,
      int vhs,
      const RWDate& rdate
   );
   Video(
      const char* lendID,
      const char* ddn,
      const RWDate& ddate,
      const char* borrID,
      const char* t,
      const char* pro,
      int vhs,
      const RWDate& rdate
   );
};

class Journal : public Lendable {
private:
   String title;
   int volume;
   int issue;
   RWDate pubDate;
   double calculateFine() const;
   RWDate calculateDueDate() const;
public:
   Journal(
      const char* lendID,
      const char* ddn,
      const char* t,
      int vol,
      int iss,
      const RWDate& pdate
   );
   Journal(
      const char* lendID,
      const char* ddn,
      const RWDate& ddate,
      const char* borrID,
      const char* t,
      int vol,
      int iss,
      const RWDate& pdate
   );
};

#endif
```

Lendable.c

```
/****************************************************
 * Library Application:
 * Lendable hierarchy class implementation
 *
 * Author: Jim
 ****************************************************/

#include "Lendable.h"
#include <RWDate.h>
#include "library.h"

RWDate Lendable::today;

Lendable::Lendable (const char* id, const char* dd)
:
lendableID(id), deweyDecimalNumber(dd), out(0)
{ }

Lendable::Lendable (
   const char* lendID,
   const char* ddn,
   const RWDate& ddate,
   const char* borrID
)
: lendableID(lendID),
   deweyDecimalNumber(ddn),
   out(new OutRecord(ddate,borrID))
{ }

Lendable::Lendable(const Lendable& l)
:
lendableID(l.lendableID), deweyDecimalNumber(l.deweyDecimalNumber)
{
   if(l.out) {
      out = new OutRecord(*(l.out));
   }
   else {
      out = 0;
   }
}

const Lendable&
Lendable::operator=(const Lendable& rhs)
```

```
{
   if (this == &rhs) return *this;
   delete out;
   out = new OutRecord(*rhs.out);
   lendableID = rhs.lendableID;
   deweyDecimalNumber = rhs.deweyDecimalNumber;
   return *this;
}

Lendable::~Lendable() { delete out; }

int
Lendable::isOverdue() const
{
   if (out && out->dueDate < todaysDate())
      return 1;
   return 0;
}

double
Lendable::checkIn()
{
   double fine;
   if (isOverdue()) fine = calculateFine();
   delete out;
   out = 0;
   return fine;
}

void
Lendable::checkOut(const String& borrID)
{
   out = new OutRecord(calculateDueDate(),borrID);
}

Book::Book(
   const char* lendID,
   const char* ddn,
   const char* t,
   const char* au,
   const char* pub,
   const RWDate& pdate
)
: Lendable(lendID,ddn), title(t), author(au),
   publisher(pub), pubDate(pdate)
{ }

Book::Book(
```

```
      const char* lendID,
      const char* ddn,
      const RWDate& ddate,
      const char* borrID,
      const char* t,
      const char* au,
      const char* pub,
      const RWDate& pdate
   )
   : Lendable(lendID,ddn,ddate,borrID), title(t),
     author(au), publisher(pub), pubDate(pdate)
   { }

Video::Video(
      const char* lendID,
      const char* ddn,
      const char* t,
      const char* pro,
      int vhs,
      const RWDate& rdate
   ) : Lendable(lendID,ddn), title(t), producer(pro), relDate(rdate)
   {
      vhsOrBeta = vhs ? VHS : BETA;
   }

Video::Video(
      const char* lendID,
      const char* ddn,
      const RWDate& ddate,
      const char* borrID,
      const char* t,
      const char* pro,
      int vhs,
      const RWDate& rdate
   )
   : Lendable(lendID,ddn,ddate,borrID), title(t), producer(pro),
     relDate(rdate)
   {
      vhsOrBeta = vhs ? VHS : BETA;
   }

Journal::Journal(
      const char* lendID,
      const char* ddn,
      const char* t,
      int vol,
      int iss,
      const RWDate& pdate
```

```
    )
    : Lendable(lendID,ddn), title(t), volume(vol),
      issue(iss), pubDate(pdate)
    { }

    Journal::Journal(
       const char* lendID,
       const char* ddn,
       const RWDate& ddate,
       const char* borrID,
       const char* t,
       int vol,
       int iss,
       const RWDate& pdate
    )
    : Lendable(lendID,ddn,ddate,borrID), title(t),
      volume(vol), issue(iss), pubDate(pdate)
    { }

    RWDate
    Book::calculateDueDate() const
    {
       return todaysDate() + 28;
    }

    RWDate
    Video::calculateDueDate() const
    {
       return todaysDate() + 7;
    }

    RWDate
    Journal::calculateDueDate() const
    {
       return todaysDate() + 14;
    }

    double
    Book::calculateFine() const
    {
       if (todaysDate() <= dueDate()) {
          return 0.0;
       }
       return (todaysDate() - dueDate())*1.0;
    }

    double
    Video::calculateFine() const
```

```
{
   if (todaysDate() <= dueDate()) {
      return 0.0;
   }
   return (todaysDate() - dueDate())*5.0;
}

double
Journal::calculateFine() const
{
   if (todaysDate() <= dueDate()) {
      return 0.0;
   }
   return (todaysDate() - dueDate())*3.0;
}
```

Index